Planning
a town garden

Jacquey Visick

a Design Centre book
published by Quick Fox

Planning a town garden
First edition published 1978
A Design Centre book published
in the United Kingdom by
Design Council 28 Haymarket
London SW1Y 4SU

Designed by Anne Fisher

Photography by
Karin Craddock, except where
otherwise credited

Illustrations by
Charlotte Knox/The Garden Studio

Diagrams by Carol Preedy

Printed and bound in
the United Kingdom by
Jolly & Barber Ltd, Rugby

Distributed throughout the continents
of North America, including Canada,
and South America by Quick Fox, 33
West 60th Street, New York, N Y 10023

International Standard Book Number
0–8256–3096–7
Library of Congress Catalog Card
Number 78–50708

Contents

Preface

Dame Sylvia Crowe wrote in *Garden Design*: 'There are two attitudes to plants in gardens. One is that the purpose of a garden is to grow plants, the other is that plants are one of the materials to be used in the creation of a garden.'

Traditionally English gardeners belong to the first school. Emphatically this book belongs to the second. For its aim is to help people with a small open-air urban space to make maximum use of it, to treat it like an additional living area. And like any room in the house it should look as good as possible at all times on minimal care. Part of the secret is to equip it logically for the activities you want to enjoy in it in exactly the same way as you would choose appropriate equipment for a particular room in your home. Plan hard surfaces for areas of heavy wear, soft surfaces for areas of play, for example. Treat the plants like the furnishing fabric – as partly practical but primarily decorative.

But don't try to plan it like your neighbour's, or like any of the examples in this book, good though they are. For, practicalities aside, a garden provides a rare opportunity for idiosyncrasy and individualism. Grab the chance and enjoy it.

Introduction

People often have a town garden thrust upon them as a consequence of home ownership rather than by choice. The house may seem to present fewer problems than the garden if only because most of us know how to paint, if not how to wallpaper. Common knowledge of plants and soil is not nearly so widespread.

Planning an enjoyable garden is likely to be a more fundamental operation than painting and decorating: indeed closer akin to renovating a neglected house. But equally it is just as worth while and long-lasting (if you don't take unreasonable short cuts) and once the addiction begins to take hold you will find yourself looking forward to weekends of toil which would not be inappropriate in a labour camp.

But it may be no bad thing if the prospect of 'making a garden' brings on an attack of inertia rather than messianic zeal during the first season or two. Plants take a long time to grow and develop. So although it may have seemed a good idea to take an axe to a 150-year-old tree when you first set eyes on it, its loss may cause immense regret later on.

What are you likely to find when you take over a house and garden in a town or city? Well, to go back to the beginning, the house agent's advertisement in the newspapers is rarely enlightening. This slightly bowdlerised version of an advertisement in a Sunday newspaper sums up the attitude to gardens of most agents (in response, no doubt, to the attitude of many of their customers). 'Unique detached residence in desirable residential area, individually styled to the highest specification and virtually rebuilt. Truly lavish accommodation, beautiful dining-room running entire length of house, extensive sun-facing terrace, three large bedrooms, three bathrooms (two en suite) central heating. Gdn.' What Aladdin's cave of hidden delights or unimagined horrors does that cryptic hieroglyph 'gdn' disguise? Whether it is a 40m walled garden with an avenue of pleached limes or an exposed north-facing yard flanked by a main arterial route there is no way of knowing. On the other hand, I like the ring of honesty about this one: 'Newly modernised house in tree-lined road . . . Small garden, big trees . . .' The point is that people rightly think long and hard about whether a potential home offers what they want on the inside, but unless they are already committed gardeners, are apt to forget altogether about the potential of the outside.

Gardens deserve better than that. A garden that suits the way you live will have to work as hard for you as most of the rooms in your house. In fair weather or foul, children will totter round it, bicycle up and down it, excavate in it and wreck its lawn. Adults will sit out in it, sunbathe in it, use it to give the occasional party and, in a good summer, use it as a place for meals with family and friends. It deserves as much thought as every other room in a house: it is an 'outdoor room'. Think of it in those terms and it is easier to plan it and make sensible use of it. Space is at a premium in towns and cities; gardens are precious.

So when you go to look at a house with a garden, what are you likely to find? Consider new homes first of all. Where new houses with gardens are available, the recurring problem is the destruction of soil by the building operation. Unless it is carefully managed, machinery and vehicles may pound the subsoil into a rock-hard pan that will drain badly once the garden is established.

This doesn't have to happen. A few of the companies that specialise in housing developments have built up an admirable record of landscaping, which shows that with careful planning it is possible to keep the ground around the building in good condition. So anyone having a new house built should make sure that the topsoil is bulldozed off to one side and safely covered. It could prove a temptation to the unscrupulous, so have it stacked where it would be difficult to remove with a vehicle. Also make sure that it is not piled above 1.8m as the soil would then become compacted and its structure would be destroyed. It is a good idea to treat it with weedkiller at the same time. You should also come to an agreement with the builder, in writing, both about the quantity of soil that was set aside and the condition in which the ground

should be left once building operations have been completed (there is more information about this in the section on the garden and the law).

If on the other hand you are planning to buy an existing house, it will be a lucky break if the present owner is an active gardener. You may hate his gnomes and his choice of plants but at least his soil will be living matter instead of that sour substance that passes for soil in most city gardens. A ready-made garden in immaculate condition is not without its problems. First the plants have to be identified, then you must discover how to look after them. By the time you have done that, you will probably have decided that this particular choice of plants doesn't suit your kind of life anyway and will have to rethink the garden from scratch.

The best way to make a start on a garden which has some previously cultivated plants is to get to know it. Notice when plants come into leaf and flower, decide which ones you like or loathe, decide whether the organisation of space in the garden gives you room to do the things you want to do, and then resolve to make haste slowly.

A word of encouragement: no plot could look more depressing, awful and unlike a garden. Look at the cover to see how it looks today.

Aspect

A healthy garden needs light and air. A combination of sunshine and some shade is ideal with protection from fierce winds. If the garden is sited in a relatively open place, the winds will be of the natural, more or less predictable kind referred to in weather forecasts. But if it is flanked by high-rise blocks or by major roadways, it will suffer from less predictable but equally damaging man-made gales.

The least desirable aspects are those where the major part of a garden is open to the extreme cold of north or east winds, particularly if these are funnelled through a gap between nearby buildings. If such a garden is also cut off from the sunlight and warmth of the south and west, it will take much longer for frosts to thaw, and much longer for the soil to warm sufficiently in spring and early summer to nudge plants into development. Also the choice of plants tough enough to cope is comparatively limited.

The gardens that present the fewest problems are those that have a substantial chunk facing south or west. Most plants respond to warmth. Of course it is fine to talk of 'south-facing' and 'west-facing' in terms of the garden. The fact is that adults are apt to spend less time in their gardens than inside the house looking *out* at the garden. Some people seem to be immune to lack of light in a building, but in a house whose front and back face south and north, I feel instinctively drawn towards those rooms that face south and are therefore light, rather than those that face north and are therefore darker and colder. Of course it can be pleasurable to look out from a rather sombre room at brightness and light outside if it is only a matter of time before going out to enjoy it. But if you are bound to spend most of the day indoors, better to have as much lightness and brightness inside as you can.

Much of the pleasure of plant colouring, both foliage and flowers, comes from the subtle combinations of light and shade. So if, during the greater part of the day, you look out over a garden whose shadows fall away from you, the effect is flatter and less interesting than in a south-west-facing garden, for example, where the sunlight slants across during the middle part of the day and gives a greater mixture of brightness and shadow.

Now here is the next conundrum. In relation to their gardens, city houses tend to be back to front. The 'front' of the house, the main entrance, tends to face onto the street. Whereas the garden, except for a small patch, tends to be at the back. On the other hand, convention used to decree that the 'front room' was just that, a living-room overlooking the street. If there is no structural reason to prevent it, turn the layout round so that the indoor living area and the 'outdoor living-room' are side by side with easy access between the two if it can be managed.

An example of the indoor and outdoor living area flowing one into the other with minimal interruption.

Soil

Soil, familiar friendly stuff at an age when mud-pies are a major source of pleasure, turns alien, mysterious and full of barely understood threats when you first try to plant anything in it. After all, a plant without soil is about as useful as a ship without sea. It follows, we reason in our early gardening years, that if you put a plant into soil it must thrive. If it doesn't, the soil takes the blame. A whole colony of plants withers. The soil seems yet more alien and malevolent. In fact, the plants probably died because (a) no one knew they had to be watered after planting; (b) they were plants that loved sun and were put in shade; (c) they were the kind of plants that naturally shrivel in winter and grow again in spring and weren't dead at all.

Topsoil and subsoil

All soil is produced as a result of rock being weathered into small fragments. The characteristics of a particular kind of soil depend on the mineral make-up of its parent rock. This doesn't necessarily mean that the soil on the surface is directly related to the rock deep down underneath, because during the ice age glaciers ground off surface layers and pushed them back and forth across the country. So not only are there unrelated topsoils and subsoils (a layer of coarser particles between the topsoil and the bedrock) but the topsoil itself may be a mixture of different types that the glacier gathered in the course of its progress.

Topsoil, literally what is seen on the surface, is the looser, softer substance on which plants primarily depend for their food. It can be a very shallow layer and it seldom extends for more than a metre. At its best it may be a soft dark mixture, rich in 'humus'. Humus is the term for all kinds of decaying organic matter that either settle on the surface naturally (fallen leaves, for example) or are put there by the gardener (manure, compost and so on). This is dragged down into the soil by earthworms and other creatures, mixed with the subsoil, set upon by bacteria and other organisms which feed on it and as a result of a complex process of chemical interaction is converted into the simple minerals on which plants feed.

Subsoil, the rather ill-defined no man's land between the topsoil and the bedrock, is not so much use for supporting plant life. But if levels in a garden are to be remodelled it is the subsoil that should be used to do the job. Topsoil is far too precious. Remove that first, stack it (not more than 1.8m high, remember), carry out the alterations with the subsoil and only put back the topsoil at the very end. Subsoil is also crucial in terms of drainage. Its porosity can be improved by deep digging or by adding a drainage medium such as ash or sand.

Plants take in their food in a dissolved form through the roots. So it is important that they get an adequate water supply. Of course what suits one plant is death by drowning to another. For some are adapted to live with their roots under water, like the yellow irises that grow by marshes and country ponds (*Iris pseudacorus*), while others, like navelwort (*Umbilicus rupestris*), will thrive clinging to stone walls. But with certain specially adapted exceptions, garden plants will react unhappily either to soggy or bone-dry soil.

Soil texture: light or heavy?

What makes soil light or heavy, or any of the variables in between is its texture: the size of the particles of which it consists. If the particles are relatively large, as in coarse sandy soil, the channels between the particles will also be rather large, and water will drain through it swiftly. A soil made of tiny particles of clay or silt on the other hand will have much narrower drainage channels between the particles and so will drain much less easily.

Wet, compacted clay soil is bad for the gardener because it is extremely heavy to dig. (It may weigh as much as 18kg for a bucketful, whereas compacted dry clay might weigh only 11kg for the same quantity.) It is bad for most plants because they are not adapted to stand in water and will eventually die: without air, the bacteria essential to the plant-food-making process will also die. Water-logged soil will also remain inhospitably cold long after the end of the dormant winter season. This is something else that restricts plant growth because plants need warmth below as well as above to start them into growth again in spring.

Another hazard is that when a clay soil dries out it becomes hard and shrinks. Since clay shrinkage in extreme cases can do appalling things to house foundations, clearly it doesn't do the roots of plants much good. But there is a credit side too. Soil that doesn't drain too easily retains plant food longer. And it has to be an exceptionally dry summer before a clay soil will entirely lose its available moisture.

Readers in the south-east of England are quite likely to have to cope with clay soils and there are various ways of improving its texture so that it becomes lighter and more crumbly (and as a consequence of draining better, less likely to be acid). One method is to plant a vegetable crop such as potatoes, cabbages or turnips. If you cultivate them properly you will inevitably dig the ground thoroughly but also be rewarded with a crop. Alternatively manure or any other kind of rotted natural compost can be dug in during the first autumn. Another method is to dig in crushed limestone. Take advice on the quantity of lime to be used per square metre and don't overdo it. It seldom helps to exceed advised quantities and in this case may do actual damage by causing deficiencies of iron and manganese. Apart from helping the soil to re-form itself into bigger 'crumbs', the lime will also counteract its acid qualities.

Don't ever work clay soil in wet weather. To tramp all over it and press it down when it is already soaking wet is to compound all its worst characteristics. Wait for dry weather.

At the opposite end of the texture scale is sandy soil: this describes a substance that is made up of such large particles that its characteristics and its advantages are the antithesis of those of a clay soil. It is properly aerated and it has no drainage problems because the channels between the larger particles are themselves larger. Whereas clay is stiff, sticky and cold in wet weather and caked hard in dry, a sandy soil is light to work at any time of the year and because of the good air circulation warms up quickly in the spring and encourages new growth (and conversely cools rapidly in autumn). On the other hand, because it drains well, all the plant foods that have dissolved in the moisture drain out with it, and in dry weather the plants can become both starved and drought-stricken. So whereas the prime concern when treating clay is to lighten its texture and improve its drainage, the point to worry about with a sandy soil is to top up, and to keep on topping up, its plant nutrients and any substance that will help it to retain moisture. Again the best way to do this, as with clay, is to add organic ingredients such as farmyard manure, compost, spent hops, bark fibre, mushroom compost, sawdust, leaf mould and so on since they will help to retain moisture. General proprietary fertilisers should also be used to provide plant foods.

If clay soils and sandy soils represent the two extremes of soil 'textures', what lies in between? The ideal is known as 'loamy' soil. How do you tell which is which? First-hand experience is the best method but since there is no way of gaining that except by doing, here is a guide from *Techniques of Landscape Architecture* edited by A E Weddle. Take a handful of moist soil and work it around in your fingers:

Sand will feel gritty and won't soil the fingers

Sandy-loam will feel gritty, will soil the fingers and can be pressed roughly into a ball

Clay-loam will feel sticky, is easily moulded in the fingers and quickly 'polished' by sliding between the finger and thumb

Clay will feel sticky and is stiff and plastic enough to be rolled into long flexible 'worms'

Silty-loam will feel silky or soapy rather than sticky. It can be moulded though it is not cohesive and cannot be polished

Medium-loam is neither gritty, sticky nor silky

Soil condition

If you know no more about soil than this, don't do anything to an established garden in a hurry. The soil may be in good condition or it may need some attention. The best way to find out is to watch what it does to the plants that are already in it. Content yourself during the first growing season with keeping the grass cut and the plants tidy. Watch them carefully: do they look robust and flourishing, or thin and feeble? If you are not sure what to expect from them, have a look at neighbouring gardens and see how their plants are doing. Or take a walk round the local park and see if you can establish a yardstick by which to judge their condition. The chances are that if they have healthy-looking foliage, without spots, brown patches or discoloration, they suit the soil and the soil is in sound condition – at least for the time being. If you decide they are looking poor, they may be the wrong plants for the site (for example sun-lovers in a sunless garden – more of that in the section on plants) or they may be the wrong kind of plants for the type of soil, or the soil may be so neglected, or so robbed of goodness by nearby trees or hedges, that the plants are starving to death.

Acidity and alkalinity

Let's consider the question of plants appropriate to particular soils. The best way to explain this is to, say, think of the plants that grow wild in different types of countryside. In the chalk and limestone country of the Downs, the Chilterns, Derbyshire, the Yorkshire Wolds and north Lancashire, common wild plants include the wild clematis, which most people know as old man's beard or traveller's joy (*Clematis vitalba*); wild strawberry (*Fragaria vesca*); the beautiful but oddly named stinking hellebore (*Helleborus foetidus*) – I have never noticed a smell; and trees like the whitebeam (*Sorbus aria*) and yew (*Taxus baccata*). But these plants would be most unlikely to occur on the peat lands of Dartmoor, the Pennines or the Welsh or Scottish moors. The plants most characteristic of that kind of country are the heaths and calunas.

Obviously plant distribution is governed by temperature and rainfall too, but an important element as far as soil is concerned is the degree of its acidity or (the opposite) alkalinity. The scale by which acidity and alkalinity is measured is known as pH and has 14 grades. A neutral soil is represented as pH7. Soil with a reading over pH7 is alkaline: the soil of the chalk country, whose make-up is due to the vast deposits of marine creatures during prehistory. The plants which are at home in these conditions are known as calcicoles. Soil with a reading under pH7 is acid; once it gets as low as pH5 it is very acid and typical of peat and moorland. Plants that thrive in acid soil are known as calcifuges and are less numerous. If a garden in limestone country has been filled with calcifuge plants such as rhododendrons, azaleas and hydrangeas, they will look very sick. Their foliage will become yellow because the chemical activity of the chalk or limestone will not only supply them with unwanted calcium, but will also 'lock up' chemicals such as iron which are vital to their well-being.

Relatively few plants are adapted to very acid conditions: far more occur naturally in alkaline soil. But the majority of plants will grow in soil that is neutral or slightly acid – about pH5.7 to 6.7. On the other hand it must be said that some plants have an amazing capacity for adaptation: the holly, beech and yew have all been known to thrive in soils with a pH range from 3.6 to above 8.

Few readers will have to deal with severely acid soils that are common in peat districts. Nevertheless some will encounter mildly acidic soil if they are coping with certain kinds of heavy clay where acidity has built up partly through bad drainage.

The point about trying to decide which kind of soil you have is, as I have already said, to forewarn you that some plants will be better suited to it than others. If your garden is in one of the chalk belts, it is no good breaking your heart over the impracticality of growing acid-loving plants. Much better to take positive pleasure in furnishing the garden with plants which you like and which will thrive in the soil because they are naturally adapted to it.

You can of course create 'isolation wards' for plants that don't like the soil in your garden. It can be done by putting the root ball into a bag of suitable soil, pricking the bag to provide drainage and sinking it into a border. Or the requisite soil mix can be put into a separate, specially built bed or individual containers. But all this not only makes additional and unnecessary work, it will also mean that the 'interloper' plants will look out of keeping with those that thrive naturally in that particular type of soil.

If there are no existing garden plants to give an idea of the kind of soil that has been inherited, there are almost certainly going to be plenty of 'weeds' – in other words wild plants that have established themselves rather than been chosen by the gardener – which will provide a hint. If there is an abundance of healthy-looking groundsel (*Senecio vulgaris*), nettles (*Urtica dioica*) and chickweed (*Stellaria media*) then it is potentially fertile soil. Sheep's sorrel (*Rumex acetosella*) and heath bedstraw (*Galium saxatile*) will indicate dry, light, acid soil; sphagnum mosses wet, acid, peaty soil; while bird's-foot trefoil (*Lotus corniculatus*), centaury (*Centaurium erythraea*) and kidney vetch (*Anthyllis vulneraria*) favour soil which contains lime. If these names mean little to you, get a copy of *The Wild Flowers of Britain and Northern Europe* by Richard and Alastair Fitter with Marjorie Blamey. It is so devised that beginners can easily do their own detective work and identify plants for themselves.

In case anyone is wondering why I have strayed off the topic of garden plants and gone back to nature, I had better explain something that seems to puzzle lots of people. What is the difference between garden plants and wild plants? The answer is nothing. Garden plants are developed from wild plants. Those big, brash cyclamen which appear in the shops around Christmas time were developed from *Cyclamen persicum*, a much smaller, more delicate and to my mind more attractive plant, scented like lily of the valley, which grows wild throughout the eastern Mediterranean. Once this relationship between plants in the garden and the wild is grasped it is simple to learn a useful lesson from natural plant distribution: as there are horses for courses, so there are plants for particular soil types.

If talk of acidity and alkalinity has aroused your taste for amateur chemistry, you might like to attempt a chemical analysis. Large garden stores stock soil-testing kits which involve putting samples into test tubes, adding the chemicals provided and reading off the resultant mix against a colour chart. Alternatively you can apply to have an analysis done professionally by your County Agricultural Advisory Service. But unless you have reason to suspect that the acidity or alkalinity of your soil is very extreme, it is probably not worth going to much trouble or expense.

Planning

A garden that is to be interesting throughout the year needs more than just plants. Even an immature garden can be attractive in the depths of winter if it is structurally well planned. Garden design by Tarsem Flora, Flora & Associates.

Once you do decide to start to organise a garden, don't expect too much too soon. People who start a garden for the first time tend to assume that it will mature magically between one year and the next. The fact that gardens don't is particularly conspicuous where total faith is pinned on plants, without the vital supporting structure and framework of well-thought-out walls, fences and paved surfaces. When dealing with plants, particularly trees and shrubs, you must come to grips with the idea that you are dealing with a long-term time factor. The catalpa, for example, a splendid broad-topped tree which will stand up to city conditions, doesn't mature fully until it is 50 or 60 years' old. And although a small town garden is unlikely to feature more than one tree of any significance, the rest of its planting should, for all kind of practical reasons which I shall talk about in the section on plants, depend heavily on shrubs. Most shrubs don't mature for at least four or five years.

The problems and the assets

Whether starting a garden from scratch or taking over an old one, the two prime factors that must be reconciled are: 'What do I want from my garden?' and 'What have I already got?'

The answer to the first question depends on whether the reader is single and has only personal inclinations to take into account; whether there are children and if so how young they are, what their hobbies are; whether the reader is likely to live with this garden long enough for the children to grow up in it from the pram stage through sand-pits, rabbits and guinea pigs, cricket and football to bicycling.

'What have I got?' sounds easy enough to answer. After all, we all have eyes. But few of us take in what we see very carefully. A good way to try to make yourself look carefully is to sit down and attempt to draw the garden: nothing elaborate, just a few line drawings of each side of the garden ending at the skyline. That way you may discover an unexpected glimpse of a handsome building or a beautiful tree on adjacent land which you hadn't noticed before, or you may discover that the flanking terrace of houses which had looked relatively harmless during a superficial appraisal is in fact indescribably ugly and should be blotted out. If the most basic sketching is beyond you, try taking a few photographs.

Take shots that encompass as much as possible of each side. Then pick out the sunniest corners of

the garden, especially those closest to the house, and photograph the view you would get from them if you used them as a place to sit out. Finally, photograph the views of the garden from the door leading into it and from those rooms in the house where you are likely to spend most of your time. From these you can begin to get an idea of where your boundaries do a woefully inadequate job of screening from neighbours, where they block off unnecessarily an attractive glimpse of the world beyond and could afford to be reduced in height to open out the view.

Do the views from the house make the plot look like a long thin tube? Do they show up a fall in ground level across the garden, towards or away from the house? (Make sure you hold the camera straight.) Do they make you realise the house looks rather more ordinary than you used to think and would benefit from being partially hidden by a climbing plant? Has its simple and rather elegant façade been smothered by a tangle of growth that on reflection would be much better stripped away?

A photograph taken from the doorway which leads into the garden may make you realise that the path that you thought led straight down the garden is in fact slightly off-centre. This is impractical since the temptation to take the short cut across the corner which will chew up the flower-bed or wear out the grass will prove irresistible. It ought to be easy to notice all these things when you walk round a garden, but it is in fact even easier to forget the details. Photographs can at least jog the memory whilst you do a bit of armchair planning.

If there is a small patch of garden flanking the street, give this careful consideration too. Its primary purpose is to provide space for a direct route to the house from the garden entrance. In most town house 'patches' this leaves very little room for anything else.

Broadly speaking, the smaller the space, the simpler and more restrained the treatment should be. Secondly, consider whether or not the space is easily and often overlooked from the house. If so, you will want to plan it in a way that gives maxi-

Left and right:
A garden in the centre of Warwick, developed during the past 16 years. The attractive assortment of paving was bought second-hand from a local council. The small lawn *top left*, originally planned for use by children, was prevented from flourishing by lack of light. It was later converted into a pool that mirrors a nearby church tower *bottom left*. The planting pattern consists of a carpet of low herbaceous plants punctuated informally with taller herbaceous plants. The walls are thickly clad with climbers. The effect is rich and informal though no part of the garden gets more than three hours of sunshine at a time. Garden design by Geoffrey Smith.

PLAN AND PHOTOGRAPHS SUPPLIED BY GEOFFREY SMITH

The plants were chosen partly for their ability to survive in a light, poor soil and to withstand long periods in shade.

1 *Vitis coignetiae*
2 *Rosa* 'Nevada'
3 *Rosa typhina*
4 *Rosa Primula*
5 *Euphorbia robbiae*
6 *Hydrangea macrophylla* 'Bluewave'
7 *Cotoneaster × Watereri*
8 *Elaeagnus × ebbingei*
9 *Mahonia aquifolium*
10 *Magnolia × soulangeana*
11 *Aralia spinosa*
12 *Hypericum patulum* 'Hidcote'
13 *Helictotrichon sempervirens*
14 *Viburnum davidii*
15 *Elaeagnus ebbingei*
16 *Hydrangea arborescens grandiflora*
17 *Senecio laxifolius*
18 *Acanthus spinosus*
19 *Choisya ternata*
20 *Rosa* 'Albertine'
21 *Euphorbia characias*
22 *Hebe subalpina*
23 *Hebe* 'Midsummer Beauty'
24 *Abutilon vitifolium*
25 *Cornus alba*
26 *Arundinaria palmata*
27 *Sorbus aucuparia*
28 *Cotoneaster dielsiana*
29 *Fatsia japonica*
30 *Bergenia cordifolia*
31 *Lonicera × Tellmanniana*
32 *Polygonum cuspidatum variegatum*
33 *Rosa* 'Danse de Feu'
34 *Senecio laxifolius*
35 *Rosa spinosissima* 'Frühlingsgold'
36 *Hydrangea macrophylla Mariesii*
37 *Forsythia × intermedia*
38 *Senecio laxifolius*
39 *Fatsia japonica*
40 *Bergenia Silberlicht*
41 *Clematis armandii*
42 *Mahonia japonica*
43 *Aruncus sylvester*
44 *Nymphaea* 'Escarboucle'

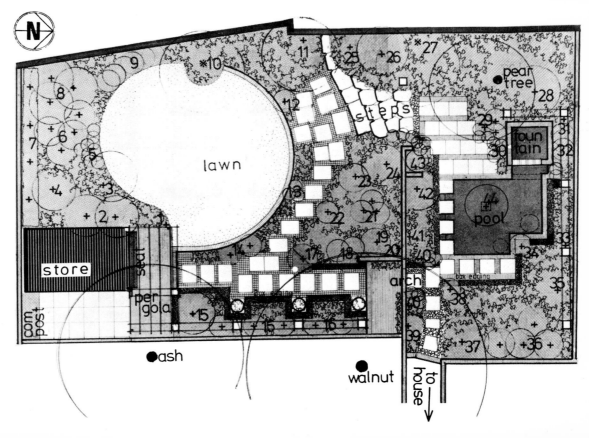

mum pleasure to the occupants. It might be over-looked by a basement or semi-basement kitchen in which case it might be worth trying to improve the outlook by inclining the space down towards the window in steps so that the occupants can see at least some of the plants clearly. If it is likely to be ignored from the house, it should look at least tidy, even rather agreeable, from the street. If you don't want to spend much time on it, good paving plus a small tree and well maintained boundary wall, fence or hedge may be all that it needs. But if you are inclined to cultivate it more assiduously, be careful not to overdo things and turn it into a doll's house version of a cottage garden. Try to make it effective in all seasons by choosing one or two outstanding evergreen shrubs and climbers combined with a few good deciduous ones that will provide a greater contrast of foliage and a well spaced flowering season. The flowering season can be extended by underplanting the deciduous

The 'front' garden is probably too small to be useful so needs to look attractive without taking up too much time. *Top left* paving is a more practical choice than grass, which would do poorly in a shady tree-lined street. *Top* the outlook from a lower-ground-floor room onto a narrow well can be immeasurably improved if the well is stepped, or slopes down to a retaining wall, and is planted with an attractive mix of shrubs. *Left* more austere but thoroughly practical: the path can be swept, the plants will need little maintenance and the loose cobbles none at all.

shrubs with spring bulbs – species cyclamen, small narcissus, species tulips and crocuses, squill, grape hyacinths (all of which deserve a place in the main garden too).

Throughout the garden, planning should establish where the sun strikes first thing in the morning, whether or not it pours into the garden uninterrupted for most of the day. If it does not, which parts are in shade and for how long. Remember, though, that the height of the sun varies by some 45 degrees at different times of the year and the

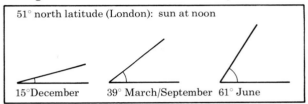

51° north latitude (London): sun at noon

15° December   39° March/September   61° June

total length of the day by 12 hours. The points at which the sun strikes first thing in the morning and last thing at night will vary and so will the amount of garden that it can encompass. A flower border that is in shade in early spring when the plants are all but dormant may yet be in full sun for a substantial part of the day by the time the flowering season comes. This is another reason why it is worth living with your garden for a year or so without doing much to it, so that you have a chance to observe important points like this.

Whether or not you can draw or take photographs, make a rough plan of the garden and mark off those areas that are sunny, totally shaded, or half and half. Also mark any existing trees on the site, not just the position of the trunk, but the estimated diameter of overhang from the branches. (Since the ground underneath will be shaded most of the time and the soil rather poor, this will affect whatever you try to plant there.) Then sketch in any trees or buildings which you have discovered beyond the boundaries that are worth considering as the possible focal point of a view from the garden. But don't forget that today's elegant grove of neighbouring poplars may give way to tomorrow's tower block – it is worth checking the development plans of your local council.

If you are overlooked and long for privacy, don't forget that a 2m wall will cut off about a third as much again from your line of sight when you are sitting down as when you are standing.

Another element that should be thought about is just how exposed the garden is to wind and how the wind behaves within the garden. Planted or built wind-breaks will make all the difference to the amount of use that can be made of the garden and to what you can grow. 'In our climate, shutting out the wind from a plot of ground has the same effect as moving it 500 miles further south', wrote Peter Shepheard in his book *Gardens*. The problem may turn out to be one of closing up a gap between existing constructions. (Think what it feels like to drive down a country lane between high banks and suddenly be hit by a blast of cross-wind through a five-bar gate.) Once you have analysed the source of the wind, mark on your plan where you estimate a shelter barrier is needed.

That brings up the knotty problem of boundaries. Take a careful look at what there is. Brick or stone walls in good condition are a considerable investment. Solid timber fences in sound condition run them a good second. But you may have moved into a modern development where the battery-hen mentality of some developer has led to the plots being divided up by concrete posts and chain-link fencing. Concrete posts may look acceptable beside breeze block farm buildings with a white-wash finish, but they look much too unsympathetic in an urban setting. And whilst chain-link fencing is an effective barrier against most animals, it won't keep out the sight or sound of obtrusive neighbours.

The various materials commonly used for boundary walls and fences are described a little later on and suggestions about how to clothe or screen them in the section on plants. But before you commit yourself financially either to repairing or rebuilding a boundary, read the section on the garden and the law carefully. There is just a chance that you have no right whatsoever over the fence or wall in question, which doesn't mean to say that you can't get it improved. That, however, may depend as much as anything else on a very valuable urban gardening skill known as getting on well with your neighbours.

Photographs, sketches, or contemplative appraisal of a garden may show that it slopes (falls) in one direction or another. If the slope is towards the house and there is no effective barrier, topsoil is likely to be washed down towards it. That is a waste of soil. It may look less of a problem if the fall is to either side or even away from the house. But a crossfall will give the garden an unbalanced look unless it comes to a strong visual conclusion, such as a robust planting of shrubs. Even then,

unless the slope occurs over a fairly large area, it will look either like a rather silly and self-conscious attempt at 'ground modelling' or an incompetent attempt at levelling. Nevertheless, it provides an opportunity to reorganise the garden into two or more distinct levels which will make it infinitely more interesting to look at and to be in than a garden completely on the flat. The reorganisation itself is of course hard work. But given that we are talking about small gardens, say 15 × 6m, a rise of 600mm can make a substantial visual difference. Worked at methodically over a period of time this is well within the capability of family slave labour.

So by now the plan, which must be drawn to scale accurately – perhaps 10mm to 1m – if it is to be of any use, will show the house in relation to the garden, the geographical direction in which the garden lies (so that you can keep in mind the matter of sun and shade); boundaries; existing features, such as trees or shrubs that are to be kept; places where barriers are needed for privacy or protection from wind; marks to indicate which viewpoint out of the garden is to be emphasised; and the line where the level is to be altered.

Fit the garden to the family

Now you need to think out a short-list of family activities that will require space in the garden. Decide which are essential and which are merely desirable and eliminate the unnecessary. The sort of things to consider are: do you need to allow space for dustbins? Do you want a terrace that is close to the house and gets sun at most times of the day? Do you need a place to park a pram which is in part-sun, part-shade, with a clear view of it from the house? Do you want a sand-pit, shed or garage?

Lay some tracing paper over the top of the plan and start trying to think of sensible places to put the essential apparatus of your life. Put the dustbins close to the kitchen door, but not so close to the terrace that people sitting outside will be plagued by flies in summer. Logically a terrace will extend directly from the house. If it is sufficiently sheltered and sunny, it will be used like an extra room without a roof. But if the best of the sun strikes the far end then you must put it there. If the garden is very small, consider paving it right across. The garage will have to go wherever there is easy access from the road, so that will probably plan itself.

Do you want to keep the children and their sand-pit out of sight if not out of earshot? Then allow for screen-planting or a screen wall. If you plan to have a compost heap and garden shed, you will probably want to screen these too. If there is no tree worth keeping, and you would like one or two, plant them so that their shade will not blot out sunlight from what would have been sunny parts of the garden. And before finally deciding where to plant them, mark the spot with tall stakes and look at them from all parts of the garden and the house to make sure they are just where you want them. (It is useful to remember that in order to obtain a certificate from the National Housebuilding Council, trees must be planted a minimum distance from the house – either 4m or one-third of the mature height, whichever is less.) Above all, whittle your requirements down to a minimum, and plan none of them meanly.

Scale

Probably the most difficult part of garden planning is to adapt the sense of scale to an outdoor setting. As Nan Fairbrother wrote in her book *The Nature of Landscape Design*: 'Whatever the size of the area, and it may be very small, it is nonetheless an outdoor environment, and as part of the out-of-doors the design must be generous in scale. It must compose with tall buildings, wide roads, open sky – the elements of the design must be large. It is like furnishing a small room to make it seem larger: if we fill it up with all the usual large-room furniture in miniature size, we're conscious that everything is too small. On the contrary, if we decide on essentials and make these as large as we can – floor-to-ceiling cupboards, wall-to-wall shelves, drawers and working tops – the proper effect is achieved. Since the outdoor scale should always stay large, if the area is small the elements must be fewer – one large tree instead of six, two or three large containers, not a dozen small ones.'

Another point to remember is that it isn't wise to plan more into a garden than you have time to look after. You may have been persuaded, after a visit to Sissinghurst, to plan a 'blue border' or a 'white garden' but herbaceous borders of this kind require not only skill but hours of work to maintain and if the time when they reach their peak coincides with your annual holiday then dispense with them altogether.

Now draw the 'essentials' roughly onto the overlay. Try them in a number of different places. Each solution will suggest a slightly different final pattern. Once you've got to a point where two or three configurations seem equally possible, link the points most commonly used with hard surfaces – not necessarily just a path, a terrace might be extended sufficiently far to get you to the dustbins, the clothes line and the garden shed. Then look to see what sort of pattern the plan is beginning to make. Don't be put off if it is dominated by straight lines to begin with. Straight line patterns work well in small spaces. Indeed, if you find it difficult to get started, a good way of providing guide-lines is to make use of the exterior profile of the house; in this way the house and the garden can be linked together. Extend some of the lines made by the shapes of the walls across the plan and this will suggest lines along which the remaining space can be divided. The tricky thing to grasp at this stage is that the lines are only as important as the spaces in between. If the spaces don't add up to a good, well-balanced pleasing pattern, you may have to rub all the lines out and start again.

By this time you might feel that one plan is much better than the rest, although all it can do is to give an idea of what the garden would look like if you were capable of levitation, but not much idea of how it will appear if you stand and look at it from a doorway. But it is not easy to visualise a flat plan in three dimensions. What looks like an elegant, elongated shape on the page may have 2m walls on either side and in three dimensions it will look like a canyon. By putting a path straight down the middle it is cut into not one, but three thin strips and so looks even longer and narrower. (Or consider the path that looked a gentle curve on the page. Looking out at it from the house it may seem all Z-bends. It is a trick of perspective. You can see it for yourself if you draw a curved 'path' of parallel lines onto stiff paper, hold the page still, bring your eyes to the edge and look along it.)

If the garden is long and narrow it can be 'widened' by the introduction of bold lines, either built or planted across its width. If it looks too 'boxy', it may appear to be lengthened by planning a path that leads away from the viewpoint, or a narrow band of planting or a channel of water. On the other hand, you might decide that you are rather happy with a boxy shape; then turn it in on itself with some central point of interest. Alternatively, divide it up into smaller shapes, giving it the formality of a chessboard.

If the layout you eventually choose still looks rather rigid and straight-edged, don't worry. Plants have a softening effect which is much more telling within a formal framework. Furthermore, an attempt to introduce the soft curves of a large country garden into a small urban yard will *not* work convincingly, though the radiussing of what otherwise would have been a right-angle, if done with sufficient generosity could be right.

A 'country retreat' in the centre of London. Before emulating it, check that the roof is structurally sound (contact the district surveyor or building inspector); get permission from your landlord or agent; warn the neighbours; and get planning permission to erect screens.

Screens are a must to protect you and the plants from wind. It is advisable to erect them a foot or so in from the perimeter. If wet soil is taken to the very edge of the roof, there is a risk that water will percolate down into the flat below.

Weight can be reduced by planting in individual containers rather than conventional beds. But these will dehydrate more quickly, so water them regularly.

This lawn lives on 150mm of soil laid over glass fibre matting (acts as a filter) and coke (drainage). In one corner of the garden a three-year-old vine produced 3kg of grapes.

Garden design by Nicholas Hills.

Boundaries

Garden boundaries do three main jobs. One is to define where one property ends and another begins. Another is to make it impossible for those on the outside of a property to see in and the third is to provide shelter from wind and rain. Fences can do the first job but aren't so good at the other two. Planted boundaries are especially good at providing shelter. Walls can do it all.

Where privacy is desirable, all the good built solutions are relatively expensive; while all the good planted ones take a long time to grow. Cheaply built boundaries are a false economy unless you know you are only going to use the garden for a very few years.

The temptation to skimp on garden enclosures because of all the other expense associated with moving house is great and understandable. But if you take the cheap way out, perhaps with some kind of poorly constructed untreated timber fence, and then begin to put in your plants, there will be a painful day of reckoning. The fence will soon need to be replaced; then the carefully established climbers and the shrubs at the back of the border will be wrecked.

Another reason for having well built permanent boundaries is that they provide a good way of extending space for plants. The town garden is usually a very small hard-working space, and needs to have a high proportion of its surface paved. So not much room is left for planting. But if the walls are used as a framework for shrubs and climbers the space can still become a lush green antidote to the 'hardness' of city surroundings.

Walls

Properly crafted, discreetly detailed stone or brick walls are beautiful and become more beautiful with age. New stone is expensive and in any case would only look truly at home in towns whose physical character owes much to a locally quarried material. In that case, and if the stone is in keeping with the particular house and its surroundings, it would be well worth finding out if second-hand stone is available. But from then on, professional help will have to be sought.

Brick walls fit comfortably into most urban settings, particularly if care is taken in using a suitable brick in both the practical and aesthetic sense. In practical terms, a free-standing brick wall has to put up with twice as much hardship as the walls of a building, for the simple reason that it is exposed on both sides. So don't assume that the brick that proved good enough for the house is going to be equally good for the garden wall. In particular the brick must be frost-resistant, and strength and frost-resistance don't necessarily go together. Well-burned stock bricks are excellent at the job (so are engineering bricks but they are also much more expensive). Stocks can look a bit tatty individually, but put them together well and all the blotching and mottled colouring blends into a lovely soft-coloured whole. If you are to buy

The colour of mortar can alter radically the finished appearance of brickwork.

THE LONDON BRICK COMPANY

new bricks, take professional advice about the properties of each product: don't buy until you have been satisfied that it can stand up to the job. But if you can take time to make enquiries locally, you may find perfectly serviceable second-hand bricks which will have the advantage of already looking mellowed by age (and the disadvantage that all the old mortar must be chipped off before they are used again). Be sure to make thorough enquiries. The difference in prices quoted per thousand for an essentially similar product can be substantial when you consider that you will need approximately 600 bricks to build a 225mm thick, 1.8m high wall over a distance of 3.6m.

Aesthetically the brick must be as appropriate to its surroundings as plants must be to soil. Here again, the opportunity for visual howlers is tremendous since the range of colours offered by the brick industry is almost too much of a good thing (between 1500 and 2000 shades). And since a wide colour range is available in all parts of the country, it is only too easy to choose a product that is visually completely out of step with old local bricks whose colour would have depended on the mineral content of locally dug clay together with particular firing methods. For instance, the high iron content of Lancashire and Devonshire produces red bricks; plenty of iron plus a high firing temperature turns the bricks blue, as in Staffordshire; chalk or sulphur a yellow colour, as in the Thames Valley. White or grey bricks come from East Anglia, Oxfordshire, Berkshire and Hampshire; and the manganese of South Wales, Surrey, Sussex and Berkshire makes them black. The range of colours available now is achieved by adding coloured pigments to a mixture of cement and sandlime and the results can be crude.

The colour of the brick is not the only thing that affects the colour of the finished wall. That depends also on the colour of the mortar. By using the same brick, but altering the colour of the mortar, the most astounding overall colour changes can be achieved. So it is important to choose not only a brick that suits its setting, but also a mortar which suits the brick.

Foundations

Foundations vary greatly according to a particular site, the nature of the soil and subsoil and whether or not there are vigorous trees or large shrubs nearby which might disturb the ground. If you plan to build the wall yourself it would probably be as well to ask for professional advice, even if it is not large enough to require consultation by law (see the section on gardens and the law).

The aim is to lay the foundations at a depth where the soil is not affected by frost or moisture movements. On average this may be between 450–600mm but could be as much as 900mm on shrinkable clays. For a 1.8m wall, 225mm thick, a typical concrete foundation is 450–530mm wide by 150mm deep with a 1:2:6 mix of cement, sand and aggregate.

Damp-proof courses

The pros and cons of a damp-proof course (dpc) in free-standing garden walls are a matter of hot debate. Many authorities state flatly that a dpc must be incorporated both 150mm above the ground and immediately below the coping. The idea is to keep the wall as dry as possible and thus not liable to frost attack. However, the wall should in any case be built of frost-resistant bricks and dpc detractors argue that by concentrating dampness above and below these two points, horizontal lines of weakness are created that could result in the wall blowing over. One of the purposes of the lower dpc is to prevent sulphates in the rising moisture from attacking mortar. If you do incorporate one or more dpcs, you must certainly resign yourself to rather unsightly 'high-tide' marks on the wall although these shouldn't be very noticeable at the bottom. Among the materials used for the purpose are engineering bricks (at least two courses), mastic asphalt, bitumen or slates (at least two courses).

Structure

Economy makes the 112.5mm wall a temptation. In practice, the finished look is a disappointment, especially when it is overlooked, from the house for example. In close proximity to buildings, as it is bound to be in an urban setting, it will seem very insubstantial. It will be structurally unsound unless supported by buttresses. But a 225mm wall can go as high as 1.8m without buttresses unless it is badly exposed. (If buttresses are built in, they should be on the owner's side of the wall.)

Long runs of wall will need expansion joints let into them, that is a gap from top to bottom which allows the brickwork to expand and contract under different weather conditions without warping. Joints at between 6–9m are recommended on 225mm × 1.8m walls. If the break is staggered, daylight can't be seen through it. If you plan to grow climbing plants against a new wall it is worth fitting vine eyes as you go along since by no means all climbers are self-supporting.

English garden wall

Flemish bond

English bond

Joints
The general look of a wall can be substantially affected by the quality of the joints. On the one extreme, the tuck joint, which comes proud of the brickwork, is apt to end up looking more important than the bricks, especially when it is made with a very pale mortar, or is even painted white. Don't use it unless you want the wall to look like something out of a child's painting. If the bricks and mortar blend well, a tidy, flush joint is appropriate. But if you feel that the brick and mortar colours don't go together as well as you would like, or that the mortar looks too pale, a recessed joint will help to tone it down by casting shadow over it.

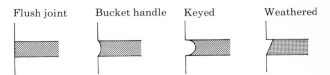

Flush joint   Bucket handle   Keyed   Weathered

Copings
Copings make a considerable difference to the finished look too, and for once, one of the cheapest options is also one of the best looking: that is bricks on edge laid flush with the wall. Strictly speaking this is not a proper coping at all. The object of a coping is to provide an impermeable covering that will shoot rainwater clear of the wall. Bricks aren't waterproof. However one way of getting round the problem is to lay two courses of plain building tiles under the brick coping, finished flush with the wall rather than projecting as most building manuals suggest.

Coping options include slate, which is very thin and delicate looking (and very expensive) but so waterproof that it can be used without an upper damp proof course. Cast concrete copings are tricky both because concrete is inclined to shrink and open up the joints (a dpc immediately beneath is imperative) and because they are inclined to look a bit hefty. Since they are designed to overhang by 38mm on each side of the wall, you don't want to compound the bulky look by using something that is too thick. Some manufacturers offer shallower sections than others. Cast stone copings are produced to much the same specifications as concrete. Options for metal copings include copper, zinc and aluminium.

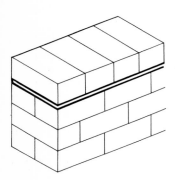

Brick on edge laid on two courses of plain building tiles.

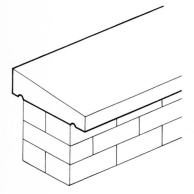

Cast concrete or cast stone copings should not be too thick or the wall will look top heavy.

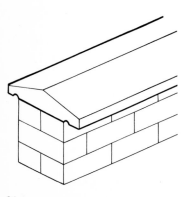

Concrete block walls

Many small town gardens suffer acutely from lack of light. A good method of alleviating this is to paint the boundary walls white. It isn't necessary to go to the expense and trouble of building a good-looking brick wall if you are then going to cover it up with paint. In that case a wall of pre-cast concrete blocks would do the job well, especially if used as a background to plants like *Fatsia japonica*, and *Mahonia japonica*, that have boldly shaped, shining dark green leaves. Lightweight, aggregate blocks such as breeze blocks are ideal: they are both strong and easily handled and if reinforcement is necessary, it can be done internally with metal rods. As with brick walls, a thin structure looks inadequate unless it is being used merely as a screen.

Bricks are not the only products that offer a superabundance of colours and finishes. The same is true of concrete blocks. The face may be left smooth, scraped, sprayed, wire-brushed, studded with aggregate, sand-blasted, tooled or cast onto different kinds of rubber matting to give it an undulating look. Some of these finishes are excellent and it might be worth looking at them if the surface ties in with the finish of your house or an adjacent paved area. Otherwise I am inclined to say, keep things plain and simple, and avoid coloured cements. If the walls are to be used as growing space, there isn't a great deal of sense in buying an expensive finish that will be covered up

Right 1 Plain concrete blocks can be rendered. 2 An exposed aggregate finish – grit-blasted Carnsew granite. 3 A ribbed finish and 4 a comb-chiselled limestone aggregate. A coarse aggregate makes a finished wall look much darker than a fine one.

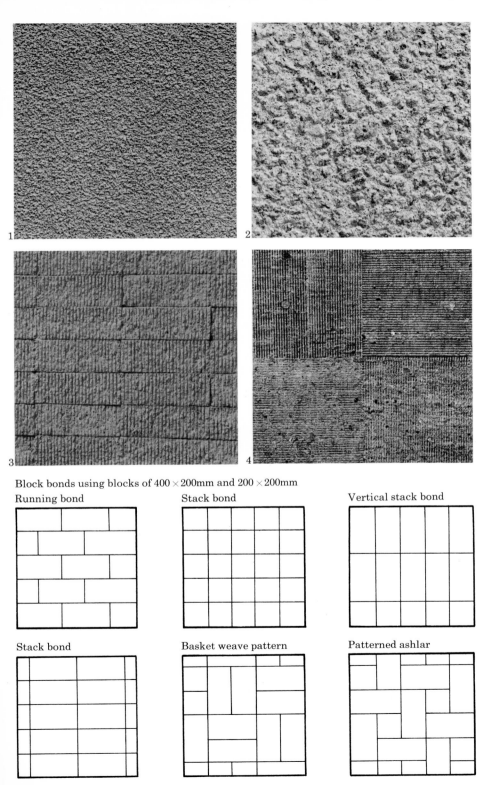

Block bonds using blocks of 400 × 200mm and 200 × 200mm

Running bond

Stack bond

Vertical stack bond

Stack bond

Basket weave pattern

Patterned ashlar

most of the year, nor is there much sense in having anything but a neutral background colour otherwise you will find your choice of plants limited. Common sizes (actual) of lightweight aggregate blocks are 215mm high, 440mm long and 50, 60, 75, 90, 100, 140, 190 or 215mm thick.

Detailing

There is no particular merit in using the bonds of stone or brick for a breeze block wall that is not load-bearing. A block is a block is a block and nothing is achieved visually by pretending that it is a brick. The jointing of concrete blocks merits just as much attention as does that of bricks and in this case the same joints should be used. Finally, the coping should be discreet: ideally metal, slate or clayware, or at least not too massive a pre-cast concrete strip.

Screen walls

The play of light and shadow is considered one of the attractions of the pierced concrete walls that are commonly used as internal screen walls, but I find most of them gross in appearance – much more in keeping with a municipal swimming pool than with a private garden. If you do not share this dislike, and if you already have concrete block boundaries, you can use them within the garden to screen service areas, to give some privacy to a sunbathing corner, or as a relatively cheap structure over which to grow climbers.

But where the boundaries are built of brick, I suggest the screen barriers should be planted or made of timber. Honeycomb brickwork tends to look too flimsy, although you might try to get hold of substantially larger clay building blocks.

One piece of advice applies to all kinds of boundaries. Don't spoil the looks of good walls and fences with unnecessary trappings along the top. Boundaries are there to do a job, not to act as plinths for unnecessary 'decorations'. Even to have the gate posts bobbing up above the level of the fence spoils its 'wholeness'; so do fence uprights that are taller than the fence.

1 Interwoven fencing
2 Horizontally lapped fencing
3 Wattle hurdle: for
emergencies only. Made for
country use it does not
transplant convincingly to
the city
4 Palisade fencing

Fences

The cost of wood has risen so much in the past few years that fences no longer offer quite such a cheap alternative to walls. Nor do they do such a good job of sheltering you from the outside world since even if you erect some kind of close-boarded fence that cuts you off visually, it will not block out extraneous noise.

A stoutly-built fence looks very attractive. You might also feel tempted by the 'rustic simplicity' of reed or wattle hurdles. Leave them in the country for which they were originally made: they do not transplant convincingly to the city. An exception to that rule might be in cases where a developer has left a bleak backdrop of concrete fence posts and chain-link wire. I think the best way of dealing with that on a long-term basis is to plant an ever-green hedge (or a hedge along the shadier sides of the garden and an informal planting of well-contrasted shrubs on the other), but in the meantime, while waiting for the hedge and shrubs to grow, temporary privacy and shelter could be provided with hurdles, wattles or split bamboo screens.

One problem with new fences is that they are much less durable if you don't take the trouble to treat them with preservatives. The butt end of posts must be treated at least with creosote and better still with coal tar. But if you cover the whole fence with this kind of preparation there is no point in trying to get plants to grow over it for at least a year or even two. The toxicity will de-stroy them. Ready-treated Tanalised fences are non-toxic and can be stained if you don't like the greenish colour. Painted fences, of course, present no toxicity problems, and some woods – oak, sweet chestnut, larch and western red cedar among them – can be left plain in the open, although an occasional application of linseed oil does them good. Close-board fencing can be protected by fitting a gravel board at the bottom and all wood must have every last vestige of bark stripped off or else it will trap moisture, start to rot, and harbour colonies of insects. In general the fewer junctions and joints you have in a timber fence the longer it will last. Use the simplest construction that is suitable for the particular job.

Close-board fencing

Close-board fencing is the next best thing to a wall. It is available ready-made with the boarding fastened either horizontally or vertically. A 1.5–1.8m fence should have its posts rammed in to a depth of about 760mm and it should be given a concrete footing if the ground seems soft. The posts and rails ought to be on the inside like buttresses on a wall, not pointing towards your neighbour.

If you want to build it yourself, a 1.5–1.8m fence should have its posts between 1.8–2.7m apart and needs three arris rails. Whether you make it or buy it, do saw the posts off at the same level as the top of the fence. I also suggest you do without a capping. It may increase the life of the fence but it does not improve its looks. Alternatively the top can be sawn off at an angle ('weathered', it is called) like a pruning cut, to shoot off the rain.

Palisade

Palisade fencing is only useful as a boundary marker. It provides neither shelter nor privacy. But demarcation is all that is needed round most patches of garden beside a street, and neatly painted white palisade is very attractive. The fence should be about 900–1200mm high and will need two rails. Palisade of 65×20mm spaced at 65mm looks well. Traditionally the tops are either pointed or rounded.

Interwoven fencing

There are two types of interwoven fencing, interface and overlap. If you want the fence to last for 10 to 15 years you should probably choose the stronger more expensive overlap in a better quality wood than the common hazel. Interwoven panels are normally treated before you buy them so take care not to plant anything against them immediately. Manufacturers supply uprights to go with the panels, often topping them with absurd cappings. So either resolve to saw them off or, if you can get plain treated posts elsewhere, do that. When you erect the panels, keep them clear of the ground, and fasten them to the posts between pairs of beads rather than trying to nail them in direct. Do not be tempted to set any of these fence panels between white concrete posts. The result will look like badly hung wallpaper with strips of conspicuous white wall in between.

Ranch fencing

This kind of fence is popular, despite the price of paint, although I tend to associate it with home counties 'paddocks' rather than urban 'patios'. It isn't really child-proof because it provides too many toe-holds and looks tatty unless it is painted regularly. That is a nuisance if you want to grow climbing plants over it. You will have to select them with care using either evergreens like ivy which you can paint round, or summer-flowering

clematis which has to be cut down to 450mm every spring anyway, or something indestructible like Russian vine (*Polygonum baldschuanicum*) which you can chop down at any time that is convenient for painting with very little chance of killing it. If you want a ranch fence to give privacy, it has to have rails fixed on both sides alternately.

Chestnut pale fencing

This can be a surprisingly tough fence – longer lasting than chain-link fencing if the wire is galvanised properly. But since it is only a demarcation fence (it will keep children – if not supple cats – in or out) not a screen from wind or prying eyes, it really belongs to the country rather than the town. Still, it might be useful as a cheap boundary at the back of what is to become a substantial planting of shrubs. Or it could act as a standby until a hedge develops. A slightly more robust version of this fence has the pales fastened to a pair of rails instead of wires.

Metal fencing

Vertical strut fences are entirely appropriate to town gardens though obviously of no use where privacy is required. Horizontal bars don't always look right. If you are to install a new metal fence, it might be a good idea to choose the kind with 'hairpin' tops rather than single spikes. It might not have nearly such a convincing 'stand-by-to-repel-boarders' look about it, but if the boarders happen to be under age and injure themselves, you will be liable even though they are trespassing.

Garden gates

Gates must suit the particular wall or fence. It would be dotty to make the effort to build and paint a well-proportioned white palisade fence only to have an enormous wrought iron gate rearing up out of it. Keep the wall and gate in proportion and in keeping with one another. Remember the gate itself is merely the means by which you get through the fence: it is no more or less important than that. But it must be constructed well, with strong hinges, if children are likely to swing on it.

Paving

Paving is a necessity in a small garden that is going to be enjoyed to the full. In a spacious country garden there is no particular need for large hard surfaces. Activities fan out over it more widely and consequently the load on its soft grassed surfaces is spread too. But a family that wants to make full use of a small town garden is bound to move back and forth over much the same routes, play games on the one and only patch of lawn, set out a table and chairs in the one sunny space. In other words, that small space has to stand up to heavy traffic, yet we persist in cladding it as if the traffic is light and get annoyed when the lawn goes bald and the beds are trampled.

This is not to suggest that grass and plants should be outlawed, only that the hardest-worked surfaces should be paved (if your garden is no bigger than a courtyard, pave it all); that a rational approach to planting be adopted so that as far as possible, the organic part of the garden looks attractive on minimal care; and finally that if you *are* determined to have a lawn, resign yourself to one of two approaches: either (a) it is merely to be a soft as opposed to hard play surface and you are not going to mind if it never looks like a bowling green; or (b) you are determined that it *shall* look like a bowling green in which case you must be prepared to be a martyr to it and make enemies of the younger members of your family.

If paving is to add to the overall pleasure of a garden and not make it look as bleak as an underground car park, it must blend with its surroundings without being totally anonymous and become part of the plan, both in its colour, texture and the pattern it makes. But at the same time, it must not become so 'decorative' and self-conscious that it stands out on its own. It should have some of the attributes of a good carpet: easy to care for, easy to clean, but discreet.

Paving also has to be thought about from the point of view of the plants. Soil must be moist and aerated if it is to support healthy root systems. So in a small garden whose hard surfaces will lie cheek by jowl with the plants, avoid completely sealed surfaces like tar macadam or large areas of *in situ* concrete. But open-jointed paving works well because it provides the plants with what is known as 'a cool root run' and retains moisture even during warm weather.

Lastly, the attributes of a hard surface are defeated unless it drains properly and this means that a crossfall should be allowed for: 1:32 or 1:40 should be sufficient.

Area covered by pavings	
Material	**Area covered approximately (sq m)**
1 tonne of York stone in slabs 50mm thick	9.2
1 tonne of York stone in slabs 65mm thick	7.5
1 tonne of concrete paving slabs 38mm thick	12.5
1 tonne of concrete paving slabs 50mm thick	10.0
1 tonne of concrete paving slabs 65mm thick	8.4
1 tonne of slate in slabs 25mm thick	14.2
1 tonne of gravel well rolled 50mm thick	12.5
1 tonne of gravel well rolled 75mm thick	8.4
1 tonne of setts 150 × 100 × 100mm	3.7
1000 bricks in simple rows on edge	16.8
1000 bricks in simple rows flat	25.2
1000 bricks in pattern with cutting on edge	15.0
1000 bricks in pattern with cutting flat	22.6

Concrete: pre-cast slabs

Pre-cast concrete paving slabs are a readily available and popular form of paving. They are not beautiful but they are practical: almost as adaptable as brick – useful for paths, paved areas, terraces and stepping stone paths set into grass – their greatest attraction is their relative economy. They come in a bewildering variety of finishes and a number of colours. The colours run the gamut from pleasant to execrable. Those that stay close to stone colours, the greeny-grey, slate colours, tawny beige and pale grey generally blend easily with plant colours and most conventional building materials. But manufacturers also offer extraordinary yellows, pinkish reds and other shades. They may not look very unpleasant when dry but

It is not *necessarily* the most expensive materials that look best: it is *how* they are used that matters most.
1 Concrete slabs have no intrinsic aesthetic merit but perfectly suit a bold, geometric design.
2 Impervious surfaces such as grouted brickwork or tiles are inimical to plant life but require minimal upkeep.
3 The strong contrast between good paving and good plants brings out the best in both; the effect may be as informal (4) or as formal (5) as you choose to make it. 6 Exploit the shape of the materials to create dimensional illusions; a short path will *seem* to be longer if it is paved with bricks laid lengthwise. (Garden 3 is by Ian C Laurie; 5 is a detail from the garden illustrated on page 13.)

JERRY TUBBY/ELIZABETH WHITING

TIM STREET-PORTER/ELIZABETH WHITING

IAN C LAURIE

TIM STREET-PORTER/ELIZABETH WHITING

FLORA & ASSOCIATES

1

2

3

4

5

6

many of them look horrid when they are wet: cruder than new red brick and far too brash a contrast with foliage and flowers.

If for reasons of economy concrete paving must be used extensively, an effective way of doing it without its being dull is to plan a pattern using slabs in one colour but different sizes. There are a number of beautiful patterns traditionally used for laying down stone slabs, but all these would have to be carefully worked out on your plan to scale to be sure that the completed pattern would fit into its allotted space without leaving ragged edges. (That of course is true of all patterns, traditional or original.) Other means of adding subtle contrasts to concrete paving would be to edge an area of plain paving in brick or to make a simple geometric pattern with brick or cobbles within the paved area.

Square and rectangular slabs are offered in a considerable variety of sizes, for example: 225 × 225mm, 305 × 305mm, 450 × 225mm, 450 × 450mm, 600 × 300mm, 600 × 600mm, 610 × 610mm, 610 × 305mm. A 38mm thick paving slab is adequate for pedestrian garden use but thicker slabs on a thick concrete base will be needed to support a car.

The choice of finishes is legion and a slight texture on the surface is a good idea since a plain wet concrete slab can be very slippery. It might be an indented pattern, or a channelled effect caused by casting the slab onto a corrugated surface.

It may not be worth while going to the expense of buying a concrete slab with an exposed aggregate finish if you can afford stone. But the point about concrete slabs is that they are cheap (in fact unless they are laid with care they will quickly begin to look cheap because they chip and crack). Anyone prepared to spend more than the cost of plain concrete could at least look round for second-hand stone, for though the price difference will be substantial you may be lucky and stone wins hands down in terms of both looks and wear.

Something else to avoid is a ready-made 'cobble' finish, a classic case of a product trying to be what it is not and ending up looking half as good as the real thing (which you can do yourself anyway).

Roman pattern

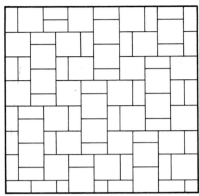

Popular Netherlands pattern

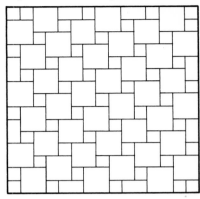

Flemish pattern

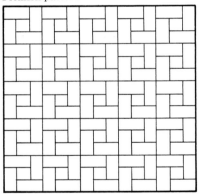

Contemporary random pattern

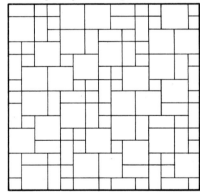

Tudor pattern

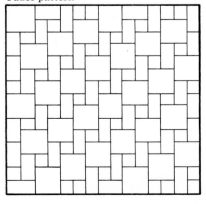

But one kind of paving, confusingly known as 'cobblestone', *is* well worth considering. It looks like traditional square stableyard pavers.

'Cobblestone' paving by Marley

Foundations
Before laying paving slabs, either concrete or stone, the topsoil has to be dug away, the exposed subsoil levelled and firmed down to a depth that allows for (a) a 75mm layer of compacted hardcore, which can be filled in and smoothed over with ash; (b) a 25–50mm layer of sand; and (c) the depth of the paving slab. The slab, which must be tapped level with a mallet, can be butt-jointed or the joints can be up to 12mm wide with stone chippings and soil brushed into the gaps. If the paving is next to a lawn, it should be set down about 12mm to allow a mower to cut the edge of the grass without damaging the blades.

Slabs can of course be bedded directly onto a 25mm thick concrete base laid on compacted hardcore and sand and the joints mortared, but if you lay them in this way they will be almost impossible to lift unless they are broken up. And don't forget that a fully sealed surface of this kind is not well suited to a small garden that is also going to accommodate trees and shrubs. A third possibility would be to bed the slabs onto five 'dots' of mortar on a hardcore, ash and sand base.

If there is no chance of the sand foundation being washed away, I would opt for the first method of laying. The sheer weight of the stone will go a long way towards holding it firm and the job can be completed with soil and chippings (or a mixture of sand and granular soil) which will act like a number of small wedges. Although inevitably a small amount of weeding will have to be done to keep the paving tidy, it has the advantage of looking much less stiff and rigid than a mortared surface and will provide the option of extra space for small, tough creeping plants like thyme.

Stone paving slabs
The same principles apply to laying stone as to laying concrete slabs. But the material itself – and the result – is incomparably more attractive. Like many beautiful things, new stone is expensive but it is occasionally available second-hand in the wake of various kinds of public works.

The types of stone that are most likely to be found second-hand are York (a sandstone in pale buffs and blues); Portland (a soft limestone) and Purbeck Portland (a harder limestone, in white, cream and grey); Bath (a soft limestone, pale tawny in colour) and slate (which can be blue, grey, grey-green or almost purple). If you want to keep a grey slate dark, paint it with milk.

Since most people who use stone will simply have to take what they can get, it is not much help to give sizes; indeed it is impossible to give anything more than a very approximate guide since even in one quarry they might vary according to the characteristics of one seam as compared with another. Anyone buying new stone should discuss the matter with a stonemason.

Crazy paving
As put together in the average small English garden crazy paving is the ugliest means of paving a surface that I can think of (and that includes multi-coloured concrete slabs). Resist it unless you know you are capable of the kind of artistry found in Japanese gardens.

Setts
It is possible that granite setts may become available through local authority work. Granite is a

superb material, indestructible in terms of pedestrian traffic. In fact it is quite unnecessarily tough for a garden. Some setts are really too big (300 × 125 × 150mm) to handle easily but there are 100mm cubes as well. They should be laid on a sand, or a sand and soil base with 10–12mm joints and tamped down firmly with stone chippings brushed into the joints followed by more sand and soil.

Cobbles

Bare feet and cobbles do not go together very well so they had best be kept to the borders of pavings where people are less likely to walk. Or to stand that on its head, use them where you don't want people to walk.

The best cobbles come from river beds or from the sea-shore. It is illegal to make off with a substantial load. They must be bought. But if you do not know of a dealer in your locality, ask the Building Centre (26 Store Street, London WC1) to name a suitable one for you.

Cobbles are sold in sizes graded up to 100mm. Mostly these days they are rounded rather than the beautiful slim fish-like shapes that were used in the past.

Like stone paving, much of the pleasure of a cobbled area comes from re-creating the character that is inherent in traditional methods of laying. Do it on a 25–50mm sand and soil bed, tamping the stones down firmly. The closer they are together the better they will look and the more firmly the sand and soil will grip them. To fill up any gaps afterwards, brush more sand and soil in from the top. When you see craftsmen do this, they are down on their hands and knees with a scrubbing brush. It may seem wasteful to hide so much of the stone, but this will allow for settling and will eventually make a very firm surface.

All the do-it-yourself books will suggest pressing the cobbles into wet mortar, but I would resist this idea. It would be difficult for an inexperienced person to do the job cleanly and almost impossible to get the mortar off the stones afterwards.

A traditional Italian method of laying cobbles is to pack the stones together as closely as possible into a dry bed of concrete or mortar and then to water them with a watering can fitted with a rose attachment. This succeeds in keeping the stones free from mortar. But the trouble is, though our weather is occasionally comparable with that of Italy, our climate is not and a combination of English wet and frost is liable to destroy the base and heave up the stones. If you are determined to use some kind of mortar, there is a traditional mixture of one part lime to 15 parts sand which provides some adhesion but also allows a certain amount of movement.

Loose gravel

I like the look of some gravel very much. I dislike the feel of it underfoot intensely. I think the dislike is partly due to the sound some gravels make when trodden on – a squeaking scrunch which has undertones of chalk dragged across a blackboard, and partly to the fact that it damages heeled shoes. A garden that is to be used for summer parties had better be confined to paving which makes it easy to sweep up debris. But those who plan their garden as an outside room in which to relax rather than a place in which to practise gardening might well use gravel as an alternative to grass. Provided adequate preparations are made, it can, unless abused, look after itself. The two most important points about preparation are that a site which is to be surfaced in gravel must have a substantial crossfall (25mm : 760mm) otherwise standing water will inevitably erode it in time. The other is that to keep the surface looking immaculate it is important to use a roller thoroughly at all stages of construction, from the hardcore base to the laying of the gravel itself. A consequence of this is that it would be a mistake to plan a gravel surface in a complicated shape or a relatively inaccessible part of the garden since it would be too difficult to get at it with the roller. It is also important to treat the sub-base thoroughly with weedkiller; common salt will do as long as it is well watered in, otherwise it may stray and kill some of the garden plants.

Gravel is an ideal finish in a garden that is shady and overhung by trees. As long as it isn't tightly

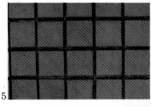

The variety (in appearance
and price) of available
paving materials is
enormous. Think about them
as carefully as about a
household floor-covering.
1 York stone. 2 Exposed
aggregate finish on a
concrete slab. 3 Bricks laid
in a basket weave pattern
with a plain border.
4 Granite setts. 5 Ribbed
industrial quarry tiles.
6 Staffordshire blue
engineering bricks.

compacted close to the roots of trees and shrubs, it can be taken right up to the trunk.

Brick

Brick paving in the right setting (for example, as an adjunct to matching boundaries or house walls) and using the right materials can hardly fail to look beautiful if it is laid carefully. All the cautions that apply to choosing a brick for a wall apply equally to choosing one for paving. The kinds of brick that can best withstand frost include wire-cut bricks, whose 115mm face has no frog but is slightly textured so that the brick doesn't become too slippery; pressed bricks which have a single frog; well-fired stock bricks; engineering bricks. Engineering bricks have a very shiny finish but the variation developed with a textured finish for paving stable yards gives a good grip.

The neat precise shape of a brick is shown off to best advantage if it is neatly and precisely laid with narrow joints. But before deciding how to lay them, check the size. Although modern bricks generally conform to the British Standard nominal size of $225 \times 75 \times 112.5$mm (actual size $215 \times 65 \times 102.5$mm) or the Imperial alternative $8\frac{5}{8} \times 2\frac{5}{8} \times 4\frac{1}{8}$ inches, there are also modular metric sizes, for example $200 \times 100 \times 50$mm or $300 \times 100 \times 50$mm. Old bricks vary significantly. Work out on the plan of the garden whether the paving can help with the process of creating illusions of space. If an attempt is to be made to lengthen the look of the garden, it will help to lay the bricks in a simple stretcher bond parallel with the sides of a path rather than across it. To have the main pattern lines running across will tend to foreshorten. Some of the traditional brick patterns are shown here.

Foundations and joints

Again, for the purpose of garden wear and tear, a sand or sand and soil base on a well-constructed foundation is sufficient. With very accurate engineering bricks it is possible to make butt joints. Less precise bricks may need from a 6mm to a 10mm joint, perhaps even a little more. Most building manuals recommend grouting the joints (pouring a liquid cement slurry into the cracks) and this certainly offers the best possible protection against frost damage. Alternatively you could try filling in with stone chippings followed by a sand and soil mix. It will allow grass and moss to grow, of course. I find such informality attractive, like daisies in a lawn, but perhaps not at the expense of frost damage.

Whole and half bricks laid flat

Bricks on edge

Professional help

The idea of hiring an architect to design a private house is not particularly extraordinary, even to those of us who haven't the means to do so. But the idea of hiring a landscape architect to design a garden may seem eccentric.

Landscape architects are members of a professional body, the Landscape Institute (which incorporates the Institute of Landscape Architects) whose history goes back only as far as 1929. However, its traditions draw heavily on the eighteenth-century British giants of naturalistic garden design, Humphry Repton and 'Capability' Brown. But between those household names and the founding of the Institute came a century of 'design' by amateurs and landscape gardeners that laid a disproportionate emphasis upon plantsmanship, an enthusiasm fuelled by the constant arrivals of new plants discovered by collectors overseas. In the process, the art of garden design in its comprehensive sense was temporarily stifled.

But clearly the demands made on the landscape by twentieth-century architecture and planning could not be resolved by patching over operations with an Elastoplast of plants. Members of the Institute have become concerned with the planning of motorways, country parks and reservoirs; restoration of the landscape after mineral extraction; the planting of housing estates and the design of spaces between buildings in towns and cities. In order to protect the environment in this fundamental and creative way, the landscape architect's capabilities must include knowledge of geography, soil sciences, building construction and horticulture as well as design.

Within the profession the size of firm and class of work each one undertakes varies. There are specialists in industrial work and large-scale municipal housing. But there are also firms which undertake garden design.

In favour of the landscape architect

It may be that you have quite ambitious plans for your garden particularly if it occupies a difficult site and seems to need, for example, substantial remodelling and terracing. It is easy to find firms that offer a 'garden design' service, but they would expect to carry out the construction work too. By employing a landscape architect you give yourself a choice. If you feel capable of carrying out the construction work yourself you could ask him or her to prepare a design for the site, together with a list of suitable plants or a structural planting plan, and then leave you to get on with it. But if you want the donkey work to be done by a contractor, the landscape architect could carry on and help you to choose the contractor and would then supervise the work, check costs and ensure that it was carried out to a proper standard. Of course, in the latter case, the greater proportion of the total fee would be accounted for by the supervision of the contractor, consequently landscape architects are quite accustomed to the idea of the private client with a small budget wanting no more than a design and a plant list.

In search of the landscape architect

If you get in touch with the Landscape Institute it will provide a list of all the practices in your locality at a nominal fee or the entire national membership at a low cost. Choose one or two practices in your locality, if possible. They will be familiar with local conditions and in any case it will cut down on expenses. Try to meet each one and see photographs or examples of their work. Decide if their style suits your tastes. You can ask a landscape architect to give a rough idea of the cost of the work you want done or alternatively you can state the maximum expenditure you are prepared to undertake and then get an indication of the way his or her fees are calculated. On small jobs such as garden design they are usually calculated according to man-hours. It is *not* possible to ask two or three landscape architects to submit competitive quotations because the code of practice of the Institute prohibits its members from doing so.

If you are nervous about making the first approach yourself, you can ask the Nominations Committee of the Institute to give you three or four names of practices which are (a) reasonably local (b) of a suitable size to handle the work and (c) specialise in the type of work you want.

When you meet for the initial briefing session, it may help to take a plan and photographs of the garden with you but the landscape architect would want to see the site for himself or herself.

The advantage of using landscape architects is that they are trained to cope professionally with all the most awkward problems that might crop up in a town garden. They are knowledgeable about the range of building and paving materials, familiar with problems of drainage, rights of light, structural support of adjoining property and so on.

At 1977 rates, it might cost £100 to £150 for a landscape architect to produce a plan and planting list for a small town garden. To do that and also to supervise a contractor and complete the scheme might cost £1000 plus a 20 per cent fee. If that sounds expensive, consider that £25,000 is a not uncommon price for a house in London and that to carpet fully a 20m² living-room, equip it with a sofa, two easy chairs, a wall unit, stereo, colour television and curtains could easily account for £1500. The comparatively low cost of landscape work (compared with building in general that is) is due to the fact that the planting materials are relatively cheap compared with hard materials.

But if this does still seem too expensive, one way to reduce costs would be to approach the chairman or secretary of the local Chapter of the Institute and ask them for the names of graduate trainees, that is people who have undergone their full-time academic training in the subject but are still in a state of 'apprenticeship', attached to a practice. They cannot be made responsible for running a contract but would nevertheless be glad of a chance to gain experience and so would charge at the lower end of the Institute's scale of fees.

Gardens and the law

People who have rubbed along amicably with neighbours, swopping pleasantries and horticultural advice over a party wall for years, may wonder what point there is in devoting a section of this book to the garden and the law. The fact is that such amity is by no means universal. Otherwise calm people may, metaphorically at least, be at each other's throats over the sawn-off branch of an overhanging tree and solicitors are accustomed to dealing with the consequences. But even solicitors with 20 years' experience in this branch of the law don't necessarily find it easy to sort out the rights and wrongs since the consequences of a population living quite so densely as it does in, say, Manchester or London, leads inevitably to a thicket of laws and bye-laws every bit as dense. (London, needless to say, has gone one step further than every other British city and has its own Building Acts, and its own special breed of watchdog, the district surveyor.)

This book can't hope to provide a comprehensive guide to the garden and the law but it can point out some of the most common grounds for open warfare between neighbours, particularly those that might be consequent upon the very act of planning and developing a garden.

There is no doubt that absolutely the best piece of advice of all is get to know your neighbours and try to settle any disagreements between yourselves. That way you save the expense of taking legal advice, or more costly still, legal action.

Boundaries and fences

Most people who take over a garden probably assume its boundaries are precisely where its walls and fences stand: that may not be the case at all. Say, for example, that a substantial portion of a fence has broken down, rotted away or otherwise been destroyed, how do you set about deciding where a replacement should be rebuilt?

The answer is that there is no certain method of finding out. The likeliest source of information is the title documents of the property where the exact dimensions and position *may* be shown, though not necessarily. But even if the dimensions and

site position are shown, if the title has been registered under the Land Registration Acts 1925–71 the scale of the boundaries will probably be 88ft to 1in (26m to 25mm) which in the context of a small town garden is next to meaningless. (Some 5.4 million properties are now registered under these Acts and no one knows what the final total will be, but it is expected to be about 12 to 13 million. But since 74 per cent of the population lives in areas where registration is compulsory, it is likely to become universal at an increasing pace.)

However, if you do have a clear plan to a reasonable scale, you may also find what are known as 'T marks' along the boundaries to show to which property they belong. The 'T' will be drawn on the owner's side. If there are 'T's on both sides of a wall, then it is a party wall in joint ownership.

Party walls or (in the case of garden boundaries that don't support any other structure) 'party fence walls' are the commonest system of dividing terraced or semi-detached properties. They are divided into two types. The first, a comparative rarity, is the kind which is divided vertically in half: it straddles the boundary line exactly and each neighbour owns the half facing onto his or her property. Presumably this could make for dramas of Clochemerlian proportions if one owner wanted to repair his or her half of a brick wall and other didn't. The other and usual type of party wall is the kind that is not built exactly on the centre of the boundary line. Like the first, it is divided vertically, but in this case each neighbour has rights of maintenance over the other.

If there is no conclusive evidence about the ownership of the boundary dividing you from your neighbour, the law might well assume it is a party wall of the second type. But if you are absolutely determined to try to prove otherwise, about the only place you can look for evidence is the local public records office. Don't rely on a large scale Ordnance Survey map. All that does, is to show where the boundaries were standing at the time the information was gathered for that map.

One piece of evidence that may help to resolve the issue is who has looked after the hedge or fence in the past. Say, for example, you take over a garden with a yew hedge division between you and next door, a hedge which the previous owner of your property had clipped for years whilst the neighbour had allowed his side to become an untidy mess. If he suddenly decided that it was actually on his land and he'd much rather drag it out and replace it with breeze blocks, you could maintain that by looking after it all those years, your predecessor had shown what are known as 'acts of ownership' although this wouldn't be regarded as conclusive evidence. But if, in fact, he'd looked after it for 20 years or more he would in any case have established Squatter's Rights – that historic system of ownership by default.

It is not so very fanciful to think that your neighbour *might* turn round and suddenly lay claim to a hedge you've been lovingly tending. Because even if your own title deeds show clearly both the dimensions and site of your property, complete with 'T' marks showing that you own the dividing hedge exclusively, it is quite within the bounds of possibility that the neighbouring householder will have an equally clear plan on his deeds showing categorically that it belongs to him.

The question is more easily resolved if the boundary is a fence or wall, because structural elements such as supporting rails or piers are normally built on the owner's side, whilst the side facing onto the neighbouring property would be presumed by the law to be standing on the actual boundary line, in the absence of any evidence to the contrary.

What belongs to whom isn't of course much of a problem until one party wants to change the status quo. He or she may find that that disintegrating wreck of fence, ideally placed as a support for sun-loving climbing plants, belongs to his neighbour who is singularly disinclined to put it to rights. The neighbour cannot normally be obliged to repair it, even though the aggrieved gardener has maintenance rights over it, since these only give the right to go next door and carry out the repairs from that side. They don't necessarily provide a right to expect any compensation for carrying out

the work. In Inner London, if you want to build a new party wall where none existed before (even if it is to be entirely on your own land) you *must* let your neighbour know beforehand, and if you have any doubt about his attitude, you had better do so in writing and keep a copy of your letter. If you are on good terms, you may agree together to build it on joint land at joint expense, but if not, you have to build it on your own land. But in that case you should serve a Party Structure Notice on him if you want to be able to go into his garden to carry out necessary work or place footings on that side. But get on with the job reasonably quickly and carefully or else he'll have grounds for complaint.

If you are unlucky enough to live next to someone who apparently deliberately damages your fence, wall or hedge, you can claim for the damage under common law. If you are planning to build a new wall or fence in a city, you will need planning permission if it is over 2m (or 1m if it flanks a road because of the possibility that you might be interfering with sight lines). In London it is slightly more complex. A wall under 1.8m high which doesn't border a road can be built without reference to anyone (except, as I've already said, your neighbour). If it is over 1.8m but under 2m, it has to conform to London Building Regulation standards even though it doesn't need planning permission (although it is probably a good idea to get in touch with the district surveyor anyway). But if it is over 2m it must conform with the building regulations *and* planning regulations, and this probably applies in the case of a wall topped by a trellis which together combine to make a height of 2m or more: the law is not clear about this. Sheds and greenhouses, incidentally, only need planning permission if they are 4m or more high with a ridged roof, or 3m or more high with a non-ridged roof. Greenhouses indeed avoid the clutches of the London Building Regulations altogether as long as they are used strictly as domestic greenhouses, and the same applies to sheds not more than 3m high and 18m², so long as they are at least 3m away from anyone else's property. It is the district surveyor's job to see that everyone sticks to the rules and if word reaches him that someone is about to abuse them flagrantly, even if that word only reached him through the malevolent gossip of an otherwise disinterested third party, he is bound to investigate. If he thinks the proposed construction is beyond the rules, he will probably lodge a formal objection although there is a right of appeal against it. But anyone who builds without permission and breaks the rules in the process is liable to find his offending wall, fence or shed the subject of a Notice of Irregularity. This has a very nasty sting in the tail: a *daily* fine which goes on accumulating until such time as the wall or building gets demolished. If the building was put up by a professional contractor, the fine goes to him because he is expected to know his way round this part of the law, but since more and more people are becoming their own builders – at least in the garden – be warned.

One situation in which potential home-owners might find themselves landing in a mare's nest of unexpected regulations is on privately developed housing estates. Developers can lay down whatever rules they like (and they commonly do), anything from the conventional but thoroughly inconvenient ban on washing lines to the less common prohibition of the use of plants which grow any higher than 1m at maturity. All these rules should be spelt out clearly when the draft contract is submitted and it is up to your solicitor to spot them and advise you, but it might be worth pointing out that you are a keen gardener to make sure he or she doesn't miss any of the odder horticultural twists. One thing worth knowing is that although these regulations are binding on the original purchaser, they can be ignored by subsequent owners as long as they require positive action. But where they are merely negative or restrictive, they may or may not be enforceable against successors of the original purchaser. (The legal rules are very complex in these cases.)

One matter that has been mentioned before and that applies to people building new homes is the question of topsoil. In order to see that it doesn't get destroyed or spirited away during building operations you must come to an agreement in writing with the contractor as to the quantity of soil that is being set aside. Then get his undertaking in writing (preferably incorporated in the building contract) to store it safely on site, preferably under cover, and replace it at the end of building operations. If any of it gets destroyed accidentally during building, you then have grounds for insisting that the loss is made up with good topsoil brought in from elsewhere. At the same time you should get the builder's agreement to take every care not to damage the subsoil in the garden more than is absolutely necessary, otherwise you are likely to have miserable drainage problems later on that could cost a lot to put right.

One aspect of inter-garden warfare which never fails to bring out the beast in us is the question of the overhanging branch and the invading root. Once the boundary has been crossed, by either root or branch, you are absolutely at liberty to take a saw to them. But if by chance it happens to be September and the branch is laden with a nice crop of Cox's Orange Pippins, don't be tempted to sneak off into the kitchen with them: you must give *everything* back to your neighbour, root, branch, leaf, flower, fruit, the lot.

Since well established shrubs cost a considerable sum of money, it is not a bad idea to anticipate the move to a new and not very interesting garden by lifting your favourite shrubs during the dormant season, wrapping the root ball and taking them with you. But you have no right to do so unless you make it absolutely clear to the prospective buyer before the deal goes through which plants are to go and which are to stay, and you must stick by that agreement.

One last word of caution before undertaking substantial improvements in your garden: it might be well worth while checking with your local authority to find out whether your initiative and flair will be rewarded with a substantial rise in the rateable value of your property. It is one thing to put together enough money to build a conservatory but are you sure that there will be enough left to pay the rates afterwards?

Children and gardens

Children and small town gardens seem to represent two thoroughly incompatible pleasures. Gardens, at their best, are works of art. Children are destructive. Still, I do think if you have decided to have children, among the things you must be prepared to do for them is to make your garden a place that they, as well as you, can enjoy to the full without forever being nagged to 'keep out of this' and 'keep off that'.

Babies

Babies' garden needs are entirely compatible with adults': a hard surface near the house on which to park the pram, with easy access and a good overview from the house, shelter from wind and some shade from overhead sun. The shade of a small tree is ideal because it gives the baby something mobile to look at. Be careful not to choose a tree with very dense foliage or you may block out the light. And remember that to plant one very close to a house is to take a bit of a risk with the foundations. On the other hand many old houses and trees cohabit happily and look well side by side. But if you feel nervous about this, the rough rule of thumb is to keep the tree as far from the house as its eventual height. So consult a reliable catalogue. *Hilliers' Manual of Trees and Shrubs* is one of the best and most comprehensive and sensibly doesn't attempt to be *too* exact about tree heights. What it refers to as a 'small' tree may grow to between 4.5 and 9m.

The flowering crab-apples make prettily shaped small trees though they can look a bit grubby in a dirty atmosphere. 'John Downie' has white flowers and red fruits, 'Golden Hornet' has immense crops of little golden yellow fruits. *Eucalyptus niphophila*, the snow gum, is a beautiful little tree; its evergreen foliage would better be called ever bluish grey, the peeling trunk is silvery white and it grows to about 6.5m. The only trouble is that you had better plant it about four or five years before you have your first child as it is a bit slow to get started. I also like the common quince, *Cydonia oblonga*, which gives delicious smelling fruits that make good jelly, and whose leaves turn pale gold in autumn. It is a rather dense, mop-headed tree.

Even in an age of laundrettes and home utility rooms with washing machines and spin dryers, it is still a good idea to have space for a washing line. There is just one rather obvious point to remember, that is to put it somewhere where there is a hard surface underneath.

Mobile

When children reach the toddler stage, the garden, like every other facet of your material life, comes under threat. If there are no counter-attractions to brightly coloured flower-beds, the consequences will be inevitable. But there is one counter-attraction that gives unfailing and universal pleasure, the sand-pit. It is worth giving some thought

to its site. For one thing, once the children grow out of sand play, it will become redundant. Will it be filled in and grassed over? Or would it be pleasant to make use of the work that went into digging it by converting it later into a pool? If the latter, remember that a pool is much less likely to get dank and stagnant if it is in a sunny spot: (the sand in a sand-pit will dry out quicker there too). On the other hand, though there wouldn't be much point in having a pool if you couldn't see it easily, you may not necessarily want to have an uninterrupted view of young children fighting over the only bucket and spade. After all, as long as you can hear them easily, you don't necessarily need to be able to see them.

These conflicting requirements can be met by screening the sand-pit with a wedge of fast growing hedge such as *Lonicera nitida* which could be grubbed out later on when the pit becomes a pool; or *Prunus cistena* which has rich red leaves and little white flowers (and which you will find too pretty to destroy). On the other hand, a wing of permanent hedging planted across a narrow garden can help to improve the feeling of width. In that case, I would prefer to go for a permanent evergreen plant, and among all the possibilities, yew is unquestionably an aristocrat. But is should be said that all parts of the yew, except the red fleshy part of the fruit covering the seeds, are poisonous. Now you may decide that children would be unlikely to chew a dark green, prickly looking hedge, but I think I would advise against using it in a garden where there are young children and suggest planting box instead. There is a list of poisonous plants on page 77: you will find that it includes a number of common garden plants. All parts of the laburnum, for example, are highly poisonous, particularly the seeds.

But to get back to the sand-pit. It should be dug down to about 600mm. Put in a layer of ash or rubble at the bottom about 150mm deep, tamp it down and level it; then put in a floor of concrete slabs with open joints so that rain water can escape easily. Use more slabs to line the sides and pave a track right round it. Fill it up with about 300mm of sand, not builders' sand, which stains clothing, but washed yellow sand, silver sand or proper beach sand. (One tip from the companion volume *Children about the house* by Hilary Gelson: 'Site the sand-pit as far as possible from your back door, otherwise you will spend hours sweeping up sand around the house.')

If you decide to be more ambitious and make a pit that is already halfway to being a pool by virtue of a concrete lining, leave a drainage hole at its lowest point or it will become waterlogged. The hole can always be plugged permanently before the pool is filled with water. It might also be worth making the effort to dig out a ledge halfway up the sides. Children can use it for sitting on when the cavity is a sand-pit and once it becomes a pool, you can use it to grow marginal water plants that like to have their feet but not their necks in water.

A worthwhile refinement of any kind of sand-pit is a wooden frame fitted with chicken wire that can be laid right across the pit to stop cats or dogs getting in and fouling it when the children are not using it. Also, a plank might be useful for propping across the pit and providing a shelf onto which sand pies can be turned out.

Pools are a hazard when there are really small but mobile children in the family, but getting wet is undeniably a pleasure, especially in hot weather. A sprinkler attachment on the end of a hose (assuming you have paid your extra charge and there is no ban on watering) will provide hours of fun and keep the lawn ticking over too.

It is very difficult to discourage small children from making expeditions straight across flower-beds. It is not, I think, so much a problem of teaching children not to step on plants: quite young children grasp the idea that plants are easily damaged. The problem seems to be that once that rule is understood there is, nevertheless, no apparent reason in the mind of a child why he or she shouldn't weave across the bed treading *between* the plants. I think the simplest, most labour-saving, and potentially most attractive method of discouraging this is to cover the ground so thickly with planting that there *are* no potential paths.

Since children will be out and about in all seasons, the ground needs to be covered as far as possible with evergreens. Ivy is a beautiful plant, both plain and variegated, and will work harder, faster and more tenaciously than most at covering the ground. Periwinkles spread quickly too and have pretty round flowers in white and blues and purples. Try *Vinca minor* 'Bowles Variety' or 'Miss Jekyll'. The dead nettle, *Lamium galeobdolon* 'Variegatum' has attractive marbled foliage and is virtually evergreen in shady places. *Tiarella cordifolia* 'Wherryi' makes dense clusters of pale to mid-green leaves which manage to look amazingly fresh most of the year and in June and July have fairly insignificant but quite graceful spikes of

Commando net and monkey swing by ESA Creative Learning Ltd

pinky-white flowers. Try growing *Euphorbia robbiae* whose dark glossy leaves grow like a succession of rosettes about the stem. It may be slow to start but in a sunny spot will gradually spread to form dense clumps.

A bed entirely devoted to low-growing ground cover will be exceedingly dull, so choose shrubs that do the job but that also give you extra height and contrast. *Berberis wilsonae*, a deciduous shrub, grows to about 1–1.2m and spreads about the same amount. The small leaves turn russet red and last until late in the year and it has coral-red berries. Most of the heaths and calunas are rampant spreaders: try *Erica vagans* (the Cornish heath) and the tree heath *E. arborea*. (That one *can* grow as high as 2.4m but probably won't.) Although ericas prefer an acid soil, these two will tolerate a modest amount of lime.

Hebes are among my favourite shrubs. They are evergreen and flower profusely, the flowers like soft, elegantly tapered bottle-brushes in white and shades of lilac and lavender. *Hebe* 'Carl Teschner' grows only 300mm or so but will spread at least twice as much: it has violet-blue flowers in summer. *H.* 'Pagei' is even smaller and wider, with white flowers in May and June. *H.* 'Midsummer Beauty' will grow to about 1.5m and spread about 1.2m: it has violet-coloured flowers in late summer.

The viburnum family has great distinction, and the evergreen *Viburnum davidii* is one of the best.

It makes an even mound of dark green, deeply veined leaves and can produce clusters of turquoise-blue berries. But since some *V. davidii* are predominantly male, others predominantly female, and others infertile, you have to plant at least two together (three will make a better-looking group) to have a chance of the berries being produced.

There are a number of low, spreading conifers which are very attractive. The juniper *Juniperus horizontalis* 'Wiltonii' is also known, rather aptly, as 'Blue Rug'. *J. procumbens* achieves no great height – 300mm perhaps – but spreads to several metres. A small version of the cedar of Lebanon, *Cedrus libani* 'Sargentii' grows very slowly, and never very high, but has dense, weeping branches.

Fill up any gaps between shrubs with quick-spreading cover such as dead nettle, periwinkle or *Campanula portenschlagiana*. As soon as the shrubs begin to establish themselves and spread you can gradually grub out the temporary infill.

Pre-school

By the time a child is on the threshold of school, he or she may also be on a first set of wheels. There is one simple means of protecting the edge of the borders from trikes and bikes. Raise it by the height of two courses of bricks. Mortar the bricks and they can be hit with impunity. This suggestion isn't likely to be greeted with enthusiam in the 'eliminate all risks' school of thought that maintains that all climbable walls will be climbed and therefore fallen off as well. They are undoubtedly right. But this seems an acceptable risk.

If there is room in your garden to bicycle at full tilt, that is what will happen inevitably, so make allowances. A track right round the outer perimeter would give optimum fun and need not necessarily condemn you to a dull garden. Build a pergola over it on the sunniest side and you can grow climbers and give the bicyclists a tunnel to race through. In any case, build the path a couple of feet away from any perimeter wall so that there is still room to grow climbers there.

But if the garden is too small for such treatment, and there are nevertheless keen cyclists in the family, make sure there is a corner with a hard surface where they can be encouraged to tip their bikes upside down, take them apart, oil them and look after them without being nagged not to leave oil stains and make a mess.

The best way of children letting off steam in a small garden without creating havoc is climbing. This is one reason why it is a good idea to think long and hard before cutting down a mature tree, especially if it has branches strong enough to support a swing or even a tree house.

There is no need to go to the expense of buying ready-made swings. A car tyre suspended on rope from a branch will do well for older children (you can put wooden chocks inside to stop it getting too squashed where the rope binds it). Small children will need a push to get a tyre to swing, but they will manage well on a lightweight monkey swing, a circular seat about 600mm in diameter, made of 25mm plywood that has a single rope threaded through it and knotted off underneath. The child sits astride the rope and the seat swings easily, though young children may feel a bit insecure.

If space is at a premium you might use your branch to suspend a 'commando net' instead of a swing. It looks like a square hammock. One edge is suspended from the tree and the two bottom corners are pegged down. Then there is room for two children to leap and swing at the same time.

If you don't have a tree you can buy a climbing frame, though they are becoming prohibitively expensive. But if you are competent at basic carpentry, you can make something up quite simply by using posts and rails. The posts will need to be sunk in about 600mm with 75×150mm planking platforms, or if you can get hold of a couple of lengths of wooden ladder you could make up something much more elaborate with 150×150mm supporting posts, the ladders at right-angles to each other at different heights. These two are among a wealth of ideas in the book *Do-it-yourself Playgrounds* by M Paul Friedberg. Although Mr Friedberg, who is a landscape architect, is primarily concerned with quite ambitious large-scale playgrounds, lots of his ideas could be adapted.

One thing I don't recommend is marking off a cultivable corner of the garden and expecting children to take an interest in the same way as you do: not unless the initiative comes from them. Small children like quick results and they like the unexpected. So while a plate of wet blotting paper and a packet of mustard and cress seed will score on both counts (better still it can be eaten), a plot of bare earth and a packet of flower seeds that may take weeks to germinate isn't likely to rouse much excitement. On the other hand, if the interest is there, do all you can to encourage it. And that means giving the child a chance to learn some of the skills like weeding and pruning – tasks that will put your plants at risk – as well as asking him or her to do the chores like washing flowerpots.

The same goes for the child who wants to arrange flowers. It is a bit depressing to see hot hands crushing a bunch of blooms that may have taken months to produce but most children are sufficiently reasonable to accept the rule 'one of each' and are just as happy to arrange a small pot of flowers as a big one.

Finally, one unfailing means of encouraging help in the garden from young children is to get out the hose and ask them to do the watering. But do keep them away from the sand-pit.

The older gardener

To read many gardening books, those concerned primarily with plants, is to come away with an impression that the active gardener must have the strength of Hercules, fingers as nimble as Artur Rubinstein, the agility of a gymnast and the stamina of a commando. The care of the plant is all, the care of the gardener of no concern whatsoever. That is splendid (a) if you enjoy being tyrannised by your garden and (b) if you are fit, but not if you are getting on a bit, slightly insecure on your legs, not quite so strong or dextrous as you used to be.

Making the most of gardening in retirement requires foresight and planning well in advance. The less active gardener's ideal garden will have firm smooth paving, accessible planted areas filled with shrubs rather than time-consuming herbaceous plants, and comfortable places to sit. Good paving is not cheap so it makes sense to lay it before the inevitable drop in income. Good shrub planting takes time to establish – four or five years – not something to be left until a 65th birthday.

Attitudes

But another important preparation for enjoying gardening in retirement has nothing to do with planning. It is a matter of a gradual change in attitude. When you begin to notice that it costs you rather more effort to dig over a given patch of soil than it used to a year or two back, don't ignore it, don't fight it, learn to slow down, to do a little less than you used to and do it for only as long as it is a pleasure. Then stop and don't start again until you feel like it. That may sound a trifle hedonistic to the methodical gardener: a certain recipe for turning the garden into a jungle within the week. The answer is partly that all gardeners, like all fishermen, exaggerate; and partly that if it does begin to get out of hand without constant attention, then it would make sense to reorganise it so that it doesn't demand so much of you.

A living-room in the garden

Since retirement should give you time to relax, it is the time when you need a sunny area adjacent to the house so that you can sit outside. A paved area is ideal because if it is laid well it will need very little maintenance and will drain and dry quickly after rain.

Before selecting your paving material, read through the notes in the section on page 28. Some of the suggestions there will rule themselves out if you have difficulty in walking (cobbles, setts); stone may exclude itself because of expense. But concrete slabs with a textured surface can provide a good footing if they are laid carefully.

But whether you are laying down a new surface yourself or making use of an existing one, do take the trouble to keep it in good repair so that no one is likely to stumble or fall.

Sun and shade

I said pave a sunny area, but it might be better still to contrive some shade as well: either cast by the house itself, an adjacent fence, a bower of climbing plants such as vines, or a tree which is sufficiently dense to cast a shadow without completely blocking off the view of the garden.

Another advantage of a paved area is that anyone whose appetite for plant care remains undiminished though they themselves become too frail to cope with a whole garden, can keep their hand in by caring for a collection of plants in containers such as the Easygrow system. (See the caption to the picture on the left.)

The Easygrow system was developed for people confined to wheelchairs, but can equally be used by gardeners who would be more comfortable doing a little quiet weeding from a chair. The profile with its overhanging 'lip' allows plenty of room for the knees to be tucked underneath. It is available from Easygrow Systems, 8 Worlds End Place, Kings Road, London SW10 0HE, in colours to the customer's specification.

If your terrace is overlooked by ground-floor windows, equip yourself with window boxes. Ready-made boxes are expensive and it is simple to make them from an ordinary softwood. Paint them inside and out with polyurethane paint and don't forget to bore drainage holes right through.

Another simple form of gardening in a courtyard is to use a table or any other convenient raised surface as a nursery area for cuttings. Cuttings taken from shrubs in July can establish themselves quite quickly. You only need a number of 125mm pots and a small quantity of sifted garden soil, peat and garden sand. A good and simple method of rooting cuttings is described by Robin Lane Fox in his book *Variations on a Garden* (though every book on garden practice will suggest a method). By the following year your individually potted cuttings should be burgeoning.

One vital thing to remember is that the difference in weight between an empty container and one filled with soil is phenomenal. Your courtyard needs to be as carefully thought out and the siting of its containers planned in advance as meticulously as the rest of the garden, if you are not to end up with everything in the wrong place and no means of moving anything.

Access

For the gardener who wants, or is obliged to take things gently, though is still capable of looking after an entire garden, there are a number of ways to make things easy. The first is to ensure that he or she can get round the garden easily and reach all the parts that have to be cultivated without having to stretch excessively. Paths should have a hard, even, non-slip surface. Concrete laid *in situ* with a textured finish has all the necessary qualities, even if it isn't very handsome, although the section on paving suggests some alternatives. (The Cement and Concrete Association has a useful booklet which explains how to lay a concrete path called *Concrete in Garden Making*.) Whichever material is chosen, the finished path should be at least 900mm wide if two people are to be able to walk along it together.

Borders

In order to save yourself from having to stretch uncomfortably, cut the width of the borders that have access only on one side to about 600mm. If you can do this by edging a lawn where it meets a border with a paved lip, you will help to reduce maintenance. The border plants will be kept away from the grass and so be prevented from damaging it, and if the paving stones are set slightly below the level of the grass, you will be able to keep the lawn edge tidy, merely by mowing it and not by back-breaking hand-finishing with a pair of shears. If the mower pushes the grass flat, brush it back with a broom until it stands up on end and mow it again. If you don't want to lay a paved edge you can use a battery-powered edge trimmer. It will pay for itself in the first grass-growing season in terms of ease of use and lack of effort.

Seats

If the garden is of sufficient size that when you feel like a breather it is a nuisance to go back to the house or terrace to sit down, provide one or two well spaced places to sit. Put a permanent seat at the far end of the garden if there is a nice warm place, or leave a corner of a terrace wall free of planting so that you can perch there. Or kill two birds with one stone by building raised beds. For apart from providing extra squatting points, raised beds will take the back pain out of gardening more than anything else.

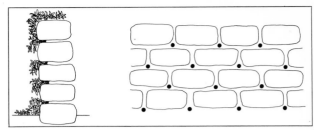

Raised beds

Ideally the material you use for raised beds should relate to the other building materials nearby: the paving, the boundary walls and the walls of your house. If you can afford to do this, there will be the extra satisfaction of holding together the whole of your garden visually.

A raised bed needs to be between 600–760mm to bring it within reasonably comfortable working reach. If it backs onto a wall, it shouldn't be more than 600mm wide, so that you can reach right into it without unnecessary bending. But if it is on an island site with a good firm paving all round, it can be as much as 1.2m wide.

One of the simplest ways of constructing a raised bed is to use paving slabs but since these are generally not more than 63mm thick, the edge won't give you a very satisfactory seat (you can improve that by halving a slab diagonally and mortaring it onto a corner). Another problem with this kind of construction is that it tends to look very clumsy, bulky and bottom-heavy unless you tackle the planting boldly. It is no good topping it off with a froth of inconsequential plants. Use a limited number of smaller shrubs with really bold characteristics that will look interesting all the year round, especially those like some of the rock-rose family, rosemary or St John's wort which you can persuade to spill out over the edge.

All the materials mentioned in the section on boundary walls – brick, stone, concrete blocks – can be used to make raised beds and a good do-it-yourself manual such as those published by the *Reader's Digest* gives clear instructions on using all of them.

Whereas building a stone boundary wall is beyond the capability of the average amateur, building a small stone retaining wall is not. A carefully built stone wall, with soil joints will not only provide you with a hospitable temporary seat but also make a delightful site for the numerous plants that naturally grow in rock faces. Ideally they should be planted as you build. Otherwise remember to be reasonably generous with the joints (without prejudicing the stability of the

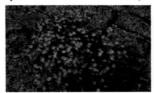 

Plants that cascade should be placed at the top of a wall; those that tolerate drought should be close to the top. By placing plants at the foot of gaps between two stones, they will get maximum moisture. Suitable wall plants include all species of dianthus *below left* and *Arabis caucasica below right*

structure) so that you can jam plants into them later on.

Among my favourite plants that would thrive in this situation are *Iberis sempervirens*, a very free-flowering white candytuft and the lavender or purple-coloured aubretias such as 'Doctor Mules' or 'Church Knowle' or the soft rose-coloured 'Gloriosa' (I find all mauve aubretias pretty grue-some unless the colour is countered with a sur-round of dark foliage like that of a creeping thyme). Thymes are good at mat-like growth and the better alpine plant nurseries will probably list at least a dozen different kinds. *Erysimum alpinum* 'Moonlight', a small pale yellow wallflower with bronze-coloured buds, would look thoroughly in character, and so would many of the 370 species of saxifrage. Not all saxifrages need full sun, in fact most of them could be put on a side of the wall which has half-sun, half-shade.

To clothe a wall that is predominantly in shade, you could resort to ferns such as black spleenwort (*Asplenium adiantum nigrum*), *Adiantum ped-atum* (a form of maidenhair fern), or the familiar navelwort (*Umbilicus rupestris*) which will colo-nise whole walls, given half a chance.

If you build your raised beds from bricks and mortar, perhaps because it ties in visually with existing brick garden walls, brick paving, or the walls of your house, you can still soften the line in places by using plants which like to cascade. Helianthemums (the rock-roses), ivies, the pink family (dianthus), *Saponaria ocymoides* and some of the speedwells (*Veronica armena* or *V. prostrata*) would all be good at this.

Tools and equipment

One reason why jobs become more difficult than they used to be is that tools that suited you when you were fully fit, younger and stronger may become too heavy and awkward to cope with.

One excellent source of advice on a whole range of garden tools is the Disabled Living Foundation at 346 Kensington High Street, London W14. Don't be put off consulting them by the name. You don't have to be disabled in the conventional sense in order to get their help, or to find them useful. There is, for example, an excellent list of tools which have been tried out on a number of research schemes at various hospitals, including one that specialises in rheumatic sufferers.

Plants

One of the most agreeable methods of gardening is sitting in an armchair beside a fire in winter mulling over a good catalogue. It is the best time to think critically about the type of plants that have the whip hand in your garden, and whether or not it is you who are getting the worst of it.

The plants to concentrate on are shrubs and those perennials which by and large can take care of themselves. If you are after a garden that is easy on the eye and relatively easy to manage, make sure that its bones and a substantial amount of its flesh, are provided by shrubs. Their relative permanence is easeful in itself; they don't pop up one minute and die down the next. On the other hand it takes a keener eye to notice the subtle changes that occur in their development.

Perennials are a bit trickier. There are those that flop and sprawl about the border in an unseemly fashion unless you take the trouble to stake and tie. That really is a nuisance: it looks a frightful mess until the plants grow up and disguise the scaffolding, and if you are not as firm on your feet as you used to be you are quite likely to poke your eye on a bamboo. But if you have some experience of gardening you will have learned that some perennials can cope without any support. If you haven't, here are a few suggestions.

The geranium family (by which I mean the relatives of our native crane's bill, not the bright red and pink pot plants properly called pelargoniums) are high on my list of self-sufficient plants. They need no staking. The deeply lobed leaves are beautiful, the plants make a pleasantly mounded shape and the flowers, deep blues, white or bright magenta with a lustrous black eye respond to a timely removal of seed heads with a second, though less energetic burst of bloom. Try *G. grandiflorum* or *G. ibericum*.

The geums need no staking but should also be divested of their seed heads if you want to make the plants work hard for you and flower a second time. *Geum chiloense* 'Mrs Bradshaw' is a brilliant scarlet, *G. chiloense* 'Lady Stratheden' a bright butter yellow. The alpine aquilegia, a small blue and white forbear of the border hybrids, has distinctive bluish tripartite leaves; both this and the showier hybrids remain crisply upright. Hemerocallis, the day lilies, grow vigorously year after year in shades of yellow and apricot. *Euphorbia epithymoides* is an outstanding foliage plant. Its bracts are a startling colour between citrus-green and yellow and are outstanding even among the freshest spring colours. It stays perfectly tidy and more or less interesting until early autumn. Another good foliage plant is *Ruta graveolens* of feathery structure and steely-blue colouring.

Hostas are grown for their dense clumps of crisp, veined leaves in an amazing range of greens and creams. They are slug-prone. So grow them in containers on a hard surface: the slugs won't get at them and they will remain bold and fresh throughout the summer. This list is only a half dozen perennials which can fend for themselves that spring immediately to mind. There is a larger list at the back of the book.

Plants and planting

English gardeners are spoilt. Almost any plant will grow in this country and thanks to the entrepreneurial initiative and rapacious appetite for knowledge and novelty of our Victorian and Edwardian forbears, almost everything does.

The privations and discomforts that collectors were prepared to tolerate for the sake of science – and commerce – were astounding. In the Chinese province of Yunnan in 1905, the Scot, George Forrest, was caught in the crossfire of a frontier dispute, pursued by Tibetan guerillas, survived an attack in which 68 of his party of 80 were shot with poisoned arrows, cut down, or both and was on the run, alone, for three weeks with local scouts hard on his heels before he reached safety. He carried on collecting in China for another 25 years.

Ernest Wilson, in search of *Lilium regale* in the province of Szechuan, broke a leg in an avalanche on the return journey. Since he couldn't be carried past an oncoming mule train because the stretcher party was too wide for the narrow mountain path, he was laid down across it and 50 mules stepped over him. He had gangrene by the time he was carried to safety, but his leg was saved and he went on collecting.

The fruits of the exploits of men such as Forrest and Wilson might have remained the prerogative of a handful of botanical gardens were it not for the fact that our temperate climate enabled anyone with a garden and a conservatory to take part in the new game of horticultural one-upmanship. No matter what the cost in time and trouble, *everything* had to be persuaded to grow. Gardens became museums of living (only just, in some cases) material.

Little has changed except that the obsession has become international. The saying, 'one man's meat is another man's poison' might well be reinterpreted as 'one country's weed is another country's exotic'. I particularly cherish the thought that whilst the British gardener is on his hands and knees on one side of the world trying to eliminate moss from his *grass* lawn, the Japanese are on their hands and knees on the other trying to extract every blade of grass from their *moss* lawns.

It is impossible to become familiar with all the plants that could be grown in this country and it isn't necessary to attempt it in order to make a good small garden. A few well-chosen, well-loved plants, planned with imagination and thoughtfulness will work better in an open-air family living area than a collection worthy of a pint-sized botanical garden arranged without any interest in the overall concept.

The most enjoyable way to become familiar with garden plants is to wander round other people's gardens and use your eyes and your sense of smell. The National Trust cares for a large number of superb gardens and all over the country, private owners open theirs once or twice a year in aid of charity. The Gardener's Sunday organisation publishes a schedule annually.

Having harped on about the importance of making the most of a small space (for example *vis à vis* paving) it follows that the plants that are used must give maximum value too, since there will be room for only a few of all the thousands upon thousands of possibilities.

Don't be carried away by the delights of flowers alone. Since planting a small space implies strict selectivity, the plants should offer in addition an interesting form; or beautifully shaped and textured leaves; or scent (not always the prerogative of flowers – think of mint and eucalyptus); or coloured or textured bark. Look out for good plants at all times of the year, not just spring and summer and at the same time, try to discover their Latin names. This is the only way you will be able to look them up accurately in catalogues and reference books. (In National Trust and major botanical gardens you will find that most plants are labelled.)

For practical purposes, Latin plant names are divided up into three parts in this order: the generic or group name, which works like a family surname; the specific name, given to a particular species within that group, rather like a first name; and finally, where variations on the species occur, its varietal name, which could be looked upon as a nickname. If this third and last name appears only in lower case lettering, it is a variety that was found in the wild. If it appears in inverted commas with an initial capital letter, it is a plant that originated in cultivation.

So the common holly is recorded in catalogues as *Ilex* (generic name) *aquifolium* (species name). But there are masses of variations, different shaped trees, different shaped leaves, different coloured berries and each one of these variations has its 'nickname' (varietal name). Thus one with bright yellow berries, known as 'Bacciflava', that originated in cultivation will be listed in catalogues as *Ilex aquifolium* 'Bacciflava'. But another that was found in the wild with spined and unspined leaves on the same plant, known as *heterophylla*, is listed as *Ilex aquifolium heterophylla*.

There is a delightful little book which takes all the pain out of learning Latin plant names. It is called *Plant Names Simplified* by Johnson and Smith and it succeeds in clarifying the pronunciation, derivation *and* meaning. For example, *Salvia rutilans*: 'Salvia, *sal*-ve-a; from Latin name used by Pliny, meaning safe, unharmed, referring to medicinal properties. Rutilans, *root*-e-lanz, shining with ruddy gleam.' Or how about *Lobelia syphilitica*: 'Lobelia, lo-*be*-le-a; after M Matthias de Lobel, a Fleming, physician to James I, traveller, plant collector and botanical author. Syphilitica, sif-il-*it*-ik-a, alluding to the disease, for which the plant was once a remedy.'

Plant characteristics

Having made a list of plants which you love, and which, after a bit of prowling through reference books or picking the brains of knowledgeable friends and acquaintances seem to be pretty easy-going good-natured things which might grow without much help, now comes the tricky bit. How to use them well.

The first thing is to take a look at the list and make sure you know what type of plant each one is. By which I mean, is it a tree, a shrub, a climber or a hardy herbaceous perennial? There is no scientific definition of a tree or shrub. A tree normally has a single thick trunk, whereas shrubs have a number of woody stems which branch out close

Proof that there is no need to depend on flowers for variety. *Left* the heavily shaded corner of an Oxford garden. *Top right* the glaucous leaves of *Hosta sieboldiana* and rich green palmate leaves of *Fatsia japonica* flank a euphorbia, bergenia and fern. *Centre right* glossy evergreen camellia leaves next to a hydrangea. *Bottom right* the variegated grass *Phalaris arundinacea* 'Picta' (known as 'Gardener's garters'). The most effective planting is achieved by placing side by side plants that have one element in common (perhaps colour) and another in contrast (perhaps shape). A surfeit of absolute contrasts will bring about visual mayhem.

to ground level. 'Hardy herbaceous perennial' is a term that refers to non-woody plants which grow afresh season after season from the same rootstock although they appear to die down completely in winter. Climbers do just that, though there is a distinction between those that support themselves and those which need to be provided with some kind of support.

Very basic things must be discovered about each candidate. One obvious one is eventual height. There is no point in planting a shrub like *Hydrangea paniculata* that will grow 1.8×1.8m in front of a hardy herbaceous perennial like *Veronica teucrium* which will only grow a foot or so.

Are the trees and shrubs on the list deciduous or evergreen? Where there is only one tree to consider, it is purely a matter of preference, but where there will be an informal group of shrubs, plan a mixture. Otherwise, if you elect to have only deciduous shrubs, they will look very bleak in

other hand, a native of English woodland, like the wood anemone (*Anemone nemorosa*) cannot thrive in some hot, dry, exposed position.

Have you thought about colouring, not just of the flowers but also of the leaves? Absolute faith in nature's capacity to weld a riot of clashing colours into an harmonious whole is ill-founded. One way to avoid gaudy colours and brassy contrasts is to set a limit on the numbers of colours you will use: perhaps white with shades of blues and yellow, or white with all the shades of rose-reds and pinks through apricot colours and into warm yellow and cream. Just what you choose should depend on the colouring of the house. If it is pale or white, there is very little limit. Yellow brick looks well with all the yellows and oranges and yellowish-greens; red brick is much more difficult, though white flowers and dark green foliage look good against it. Stone is an excellent foil for almost anything.

Think too about the time of flowering. A high proportion of herbaceous plants is apt to explode in a riot of colour over a period of two or three summer months. Shrubs give much more leeway. Mahonias, viburnums, chaenomeles, daphnes, camellias and witch hazel are just a few of a large number of shrubs that flower in the winter months. There are many more that flower in the summer. By a bit of judicious juggling you can, if you want, have something in flower during most of the year.

If in five years' time a monochrome photograph of your garden shows no noticeable distinction between one shrub and the next, it suggests you didn't stop to think about the contrast in leaf colours. They vary enormously from bluish-grey and silver, to yellowish-green and all the way to the darkest bottle colours. They vary too because some are deeply veined, others not; some are shiny, some are dull; some have velvety undersides of yellowish brown or silvery white; some are velvety all over; many combine two or more colours in a single leaf; others turn from one distinct colour in spring to an entirely different one in autumn.

The intensity of colour of a particular shrub will vary too, according to the size of leaf, its shape and the density of its foliage. Some of the very finely

winter; and if you opt entirely for evergreens the garden is going to look pretty dark and overpowering throughout the year.

Do you know whether the plant prefers sun or is happier in shade, or will it tolerate most situations? This factor is more crucial to some plants than others. Imagine, for example, the preference of plants that originated in Mediterranean coastal regions. Not many of these would take kindly to being allocated to some damp shady corner; on the cut maples have leaves that are almost wine-coloured. But the impression of the colour is quite luminous compared to the almost black-red of a mature copper beech tree whose foliage is so dense that the light can hardly penetrate it and whose leaves are a rounded, even shape. And as if all that wasn't enough to think about, there is the shape of the tree or shrub itself to consider. Just look at the contrast in forms that occur within a single plant group as shown below.

Take two of the pear trees, *Pyrus salicifolia* 'Pendula' and *P. communis* 'Beech Hill'

Or three of the viburnums: *V.* × *burkwoodii*, *V. davidii* and *V. tomentosum* 'Lanarth'

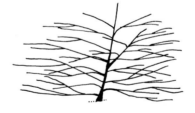

Or two of the cotoneasters: *C. hybrida* Donard Gem and *C. Simonsii*

Some of the most common shapes are classified as follows:

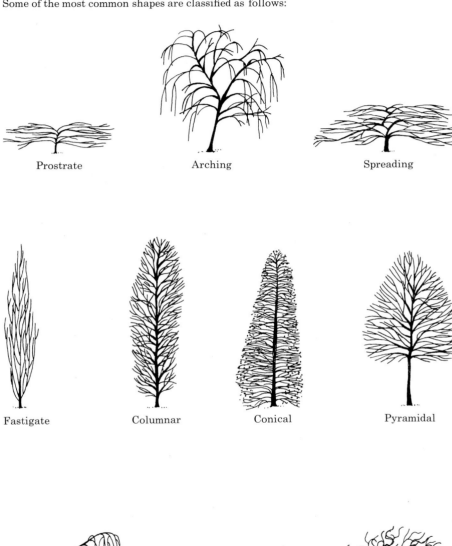

Prostrate

Arching

Spreading

Fastigate

Columnar

Conical

Pyramidal

Weeping

Mop-headed

Contorted

There are situations when it would be absolutely appropriate to plant nothing but one particular shape of tree (an avenue of balsam poplars would look superb beside a long straight drive). If you have opted for a completely regular, angular ground pattern, you may decide that it would look best with a formal pattern of clipped box, privet or yew. But if you visualise much more informal groups of shrubs, try to make use of these contrasts in form, leaf shape, leaf and flower colour. It is a bit like setting a stage. There is a backdrop behind a set on which are clearly seen individual props. Thus the taller shrubs with small, densely packed leaves become the rather solid-looking backdrop against which shrubs with bolder characteristics stand out like the structure of a set, with points of colour from herbaceous plants providing foreground 'props'. 'The best associations', wrote Sylvia Crowe in *Garden Design,* 'are between plants which have one element in common and another contrasted. Complete contrast in all elements can be used for special emphasis, but repeated too often the effect is restless, lacking the unity given by a connecting link of similarity.' That linking element might, for example, be similarity of colour set off against contrast in leaf shape and texture.

Try not to be seduced, as too many commercial hybridisers are, by the idea that bigger, bolder, brighter necessarily means better. A character in Angus Wilson's novel *The Middle Age of Mrs Eliot* says of the rhododendrons developed by the manager of his nursery: 'It is unfortunate, of course, that Tim's additions to English horticulture should be of such extreme hideousness, but then that only ensures a greater market for them.' The more hideous the product, the more readily available it seems to become so that we end up with shocking-pink roses on the supermarket shelves in take-away boxes whilst the real treasures, like *Rosa rubrifolia* are confined to the good nurseries.

One interesting way of avoiding 'extreme hideousness' is to avoid garden hybrids (except those you have tested with your own eyes and long to grow) and choose instead species plants. They are available from good nurseries in just the same way as hybrids and having been grown from selected stock should produce strong healthy plants. But in every essential way they will have those qualities of balance and proportion which are intrinsic to the wild plant. A book which gives an excellent introduction to European as well as native species is Oleg Polunin's *Trees and Bushes of Europe*.

Above all, make use of the walls. You may double, treble, even quadruple the scope of the smallest garden if you clothe the walls with climbers, fruiting trees or shrubs that either lend themselves to being pulled back flat by ties (the morello cherry) or tolerate being clipped back flat (like the chaenomeles).

Vegetables and fruit

It is not realistic to hope that a family can live off a small town garden to any useful extent unless prepared to dispense with ornamental plants altogether. A space of about 84m² would be necessary to supply a family of four with summer and winter vegetables. Even to make regular use of a variety of herbs means setting aside a substantial chunk of border. But a salad flavoured with fresh parsley, mint and sorrel, or tomato soup flavoured with fresh basil is such a pleasure that it is a good idea to choose four, or at most six, favourite herbs and give them sufficient space to grow into a really worthwhile crop.

The space-to-crop ratio of the tomato makes it a useful town garden plant. 'Outdoor Girl' and 'Gardener's Delight' and the yellow fruiting 'Golden Sunrise' all have a good flavour, crop well and are happy out of doors. To make sure that the maximum amount of sun reaches them, it is just as well to keep them out of the border, neatly staked and tied in their own containers. But feed them and water them regularly since they must not be allowed to dry out.

One good way to combine, as it were, business with pleasure in a small space is to devote the 'vertical' part of the garden – the boundary walls and fences – to fruit-trees. By pruning and training

them to grow as cordons, espaliers, half standards and so on, you can pin them back into formal patterns that occupy minimal space and look immensely attractive. The more extreme shapes tend to limit the production of fruit, nevertheless they should produce a worthwhile crop.

Apple trees that do well in London include 'Laxton's Superb', 'Beauty of Bath', 'Allington Pippin', 'Cox's Orange Pippin', 'Ellison's Orange', 'Worcester Pearmain' and 'Sturmer Pippin'. The pears 'Doyenné du Comice' and 'Conference' are also satisfactory. But neither apples or pears will survive frost and they dislike damp, so the drier, warmer cities of the south and south-east will have a better chance of producing good fruit.

Apples, pears, peaches ('Moorpark' is reliable) and plums need a warm, south-facing position, but morello cherries and red currants can both be grown against a north-facing wall.

Invest in good stock from a reliable nursery. John Scott of Merriott offers an enormous choice

Don't confine plants strictly to flower-beds. Many will thrive in paving. *Above left* ivy, *Campanula portenschlagiana* and lily of the valley all do well in shade; *top* a hebe will need a sunny site. *Above* containers can be planted with bulbs for spring flowering and then with annuals for summer flowering. Petunias have a long season if the seed heads are picked off.

of fruits, with young apple and pear plants already pruned into the various artificial shapes. It also supplies an exceptionally informative catalogue.

Preparation of the ground

Do not plant anything until the ground is well prepared. If necessary let a whole season go by without planting a thing, rather than be in too much of a hurry. For plants put into well-prepared ground will have a much better chance of success; and subsequent maintenance will be reduced. The first stage is to clean the ground. Dig out all the weeds and use the annuals to start a compost heap. Dig out every last bit of rubbish; be it stones, bricks, builders' rubble, old bicycle wheels, bedsteads or air-raid shelters. If disposing of it is a problem, hire a skip. It may seem pricey, but perhaps not compared to the wear and tear on your car if you try to carry the rubbish away to the tip bagged up in the boot.

When the rubbish has been cleaned out, dig over the soil thoroughly, either the depth of a spade or to double that depth. But if you dig to double the depth, don't mix up the topsoil and subsoil. During the digging process, try to add in a good dose of well-rotted organic matter – manure, compost, spent hops or leaf mould – that will help to feed the soil, together with a small quantity of a general compound chemical fertiliser to feed the plants.

Planting: where and how

Don't allow garden conventions to cramp your style when it comes to planting. Plants need not be confined rigidly within the boundaries of a flower-bed; allow them to spill over the edges, particularly if the bed is surrounded by paving. Plant tough spreading rock plants in the crevices between paving slabs. If the paving abuts a wall or fence, lift a slab or two, prepare a rich pocket of soil and plant a climber. Invest in one or two good terracotta containers for the edge of the area where you sit out and choose plants for them that are rich in colour or fragrance. Powder-blue petunias, scarlet or white pelargoniums or the fragile *Viola cornuta* will all flower for weeks on end if the

seed heads are picked off as the flowers die. Scented plants small enough for a container include primroses, the species crocuses (not the fat Dutch hybrids), *Helichrysum angustifolium* (a silver-leaved plant which smells of curry) or if that is a little too exotic, rosemary, lavender, lemon balm. If the pot is large enough, try white *Lilium regale*, which Ernest Wilson collected at his peril.

There is not enough room in this book to go into the details of planting and maintenance. There is room to say that it is well worth getting to know the most basic rules thoroughly: such as digging a hole an adequate size for the root ball; taking care not to disturb the roots; ensuring that the plant has been pressed firmly into the ground; watering it adequately after planting. All this is fully explained in numerous gardening books including the excellent *Penguin Book of Basic Gardening* by Alan Gemmell.

I have hardly mentioned lawns, except to suggest that they may be more trouble than they are worth in a small town garden. If you are hell-bent on perfection, I strongly advise getting a specialist book out of the library and reading it thoroughly. If you merely want a soft as opposed to a hard play area for your family then common sense and recourse to *Basic Gardening* will see you through. Essentially you need a flat, well-drained site with 70 or 100mm of good topsoil. Onto that you sow a proprietary brand of basic lawn seed (70g per square metre) in the autumn or spring. The new lawn shouldn't be mown until it is 75mm high. After that it has to be mown regularly. In a country garden I think it would be worth going to immense trouble to make a good lawn, but in a town, where shade, or dripping from overhanging trees, or heavy wear will all contribute to its fall from grace, I would seriously think about opting for paving and crevice-loving plants.

Degradable kitchen waste makes good compost. Make your own bin in wood or strong wire mesh (air must get to the compost to enable it to break down) or buy a ready-made bin like the Rotocrop *below*. Add compost to the soil during the spring dig or any other major digging session.

Case history 1

Pat and John Wardroper live in St Paul's Road, Islington, north London. They built their house, a 1963/4 addition to an 1837 terrace at a time when their three children were aged between six and nine. The land to the west of them had been built over before the war but was devastated by bombing. A 450mm layer of rubble had come to rest on what was to become their 21 × 5.5m garden.

The Wardropers brought a total of four or five years' gardening experience at their previous home to the task of making something of their new site. There was, they decided, only one way to set about it: start at the back of the house and push out the frontiers of broken brick and rubbish as they went along. The house and garden lie due north/south, the back of the house facing north, the length of the garden. This meant that the area immediately behind the house, which is three storeys high, would never get much sun. So they resolved to pave it and save themselves the fruitless struggle of persuading more than a few shade-loving plants to grow there.

They found some York paving when digging in the garden to try and get at the soil and bought the rest. John Wardroper laid it himself in a bed of sand, without mortar. He had no experience of the job at the time and it took weeks of painstaking levelling, lifting and readjustment. The result is far more attractive than the work done later at the opposite end of the garden by a professional builder who did use mortar. To begin with, they regretted leaving open the crevices between the stones because of the influx of weeds. But after some years of tenacious weeding, these disappeared and now the cracks are filled with campanulas, periwinkles and (by choice) dead nettle.

Pat Wardroper has no clear recollection of how they planned the garden, although she does remember that they tried to get some ideas down on paper. The quantity of rubble in the garden was such that either it had to go, which was expensive, or it had to stay and be made useful. In the event, all but one lorry-load stayed and was used to raise the central part of the garden on which they laid their lawn. The 300mm rise occurs just beyond the garden door, in line with the first buttress of a brick wall which had been built along the west side of the garden at the same time as the house.

In the process of rearranging the rubble, John Wardroper also excavated quantities of good quality soil, which he found 460mm down. The district had once been an area of market gardens. By systematically 'trenching', digging away a section of rubble, shovelling out the good soil, and filling up that section with the neighbouring layer of rubble and so on, he gradually worked his way to the far end of what was to become the lawn.

Pat Wardroper wanted one tree to provide interest throughout the year and occupy a principal position. She chose the crab apple *Malus* 'John Downie' and planted it to the left of the sight line from the living-room window, close to the rise between the paved area and the lawn. It has white flowers in early summer and they use its conical orange and red fruits to make jelly and wine. Its growth is open, so that it casts only dappled shade and is easy to see through.

John Wardroper took charge of laying the lawn and the path which crosses it on the eastern side. The path, which aligns with the steps that lead down from the living room balcony at the back of the house, follows the shape of the west-facing border. The border partially hides what was to become the eating and drinking area at the far end of the garden. But the tendency of the plants to grow towards the afternoon sun makes the Wardropers wonder if the border wasn't a bit too wide to begin with.

Before planting the garden Pat Wardroper had collected notes on what she reckoned were 'good London plants' particularly shrubs, because of their year-round value. On the whole she is pleased with what she chose except for her second *Choisya ternata*, the Mexican orange blossom: 'There really is only room for one in a small garden.' Ten or twelve years after planting, some of the shrubs, such as a ceanothus and a cytisus, have stretched up towards the light ('the books never tell you what to do to stop that sort of thing') becoming very leggy and tree-like and she

is having to underplant in some cases to try to fill out the gaps.

On the opposite side of the garden she avoided the cliché of just another border and took the grass almost as far as the wall, leaving only enough space to plant climbers, wall shrubs and a couple of interesting trees, *Robinia pseudoacacia* 'Frisia' and *Acer negundo* 'Variegatum'.

The garden got no further than the end of the lawn for several years. Then five years ago, they decided to get the north end of the garden sorted out once and for all and Pat Wardroper called in a designer whose name she had seen in a gardening magazine. The designer planned a paved area, large enough to take a table and four chairs comfortably. She also left room for a south-facing bed that is filled with sun-loving plants such as a fan-trained peach, rock-roses and *Phlomis fruticosa*. A small wooden garden shed houses bicycles and garden tools (now rationalised to a spade and garden fork). The Wardropers were happy with the scheme. Their only reservations were that they found rainwater standing in lakes on the paving when it was first laid and had to get the builder to come back and drill drainage holes. They also disliked the look of mortar between the stone slabs; but as a defence against weeds it is invaluable.

If she had a chance to start all over again, Mrs Wardroper thinks she would have been much more inclined to try and foreshorten the view of the garden from the house by making one or two bold lines of planting across it from east to west. It would also have provided people sitting in the paved area with a little more privacy. She doesn't think it was an ideal garden for growing children. 'I suppose we didn't really make much special provision for them. If we had wanted a completely childproof garden – one that would stand up to constant football games – the best thing would have been to pave the whole area and simply plant a few trees. But we felt that would have been rather lacking in interest in the long term.'

She also wishes she had chosen repeat-flowering roses in every case. 'In a small garden, everything really does have to work extra hard.' Nobody, she

says, who wants a minimal-care garden should have anything to do with a lawn, and everybody would do well to organise a water supply in the garden itself. 'We were lucky: there is a tap just inside the garden door. I can't think what it would be like if we had to connect the hose to the kitchen tap every time.' The 1976 drought added considerably to the time Pat Wardroper spent in her garden but in a 'normal' year, she thinks it would occupy not more than three to four hours' work each week.

Case history 2

Mr and Mrs Ronald Palin moved to their small, early nineteenth-century terrace London house in 1961. At that time both of them had some experience of gardening but they had never before started a garden from scratch. Their new garden, at the back of the house, was 15 × 5m, bounded by brick walls. It sloped up, away from the house, in a west-south-westerly direction. Part of it was occupied by a wooden annexe that housed the bathroom beside the brick-built outside lavatory. Both structures were demolished. There was also a dense covering of coarse, tall grass and an ugly and mutilated sycamore tree that stole all the light from their kitchen. That was removed too. But evidently the garden had been cultivated once for there was also a small gingko tree, one or two climbing roses whose names they never discovered, and a thriving forsythia bush at the far end.

Although at an early stage the Palins decided they needed professional help to construct the garden, the design was their own. The slope from the house towards the far end of the garden looked unsatisfactory. During heavy rain, soil was washed down towards the basement kitchen which has a window overlooking the garden. So it was decided to level and pave a substantial area at the back of the house and use the excess subsoil from this operation to push back and raise the rest of the garden by about 600mm.

They bought York stone paving within two blocks of the house after spotting local authority workmen digging up a pavement. The slabs were laid the full width of the plot like wall-to-wall carpeting. 'We were sure it would look more spacious that way and in any case, we were determined that everything about the design should be as simple as possible.' The paving was laid according to a ground plan which they worked out themselves after deciding on a number of plants which were to become permanent features of the courtyard. These included a wistaria which climbs a column to a first-floor extension; a jasmine, honeysuckle and a vine with purple grapes which thrives despite spending all but the latter part of the day in shade. In each case a space was left between paving stones, approximately 350 × 350mm and a rich pocket of soil prepared for each plant.

This essentially simple scheme had the effect of making the garden seem much wider and more spacious than before. The only mildly adverse effect was that by raising a substantial part of the garden they lost 600mm in height from the boundary walls, so they added on some trellis and built up the brick wall along the south side of the courtyard to complete their privacy from the neighbours on that side.

The central pool of colour in the garden is a lawn 3 × 9m which is as close to emerald perfection as one is likely to see and is, according to Ronald Palin, without question the most cosseted

lawn in London. Round the other three sides of the lawn are borders: the one on the right is 1.2m wide because it faces south-east and gets most of the sun; the one on the left is 1m wide; while the bed at the end is 1.5m wide to allow room to mass shrubs leading up to the trees. The borders are edged with a two-brick lip and there is a one-brick margin, a 'mowing stone', all the way round the lawn so that the cutter can get right to the edge of the grass.

The next step was to furnish the garden. They used a good nursery, drew up and submitted a sketch plan, indicated the direction in which the garden lay and gave an idea of the kind of plants they wanted (predominantly shrubs and perennials, since they both had professional careers and neither of them had much time to spare).

The nursery worked out a scheme and provided the plants which were put in one vile and wet November day. Fortunately, the lawn, which was due to be turfed, was still only staked out at that stage or it would have been wrecked.

Apart from its west-south-westerly aspect, the main factors which had, and still have, to be considered in terms of light and shade were four substantial neighbouring trees at the far end: a fig, a pear, a sycamore and a huge bay tree. The rising sun lights up the far right-hand corner of the garden, works its way along the right-hand bed, into the courtyard and then along the left-hand border. But for the fig tree, that border would receive an almost equal amount of sun. As it is, the far left corner gets none at all.

Mrs Palin became adept at taking her own cuttings and raising new plants ready to replace old ones as their performance tailed off. She has three or four groups of cuttings in pots arranged on white wire jardinières and a table in the courtyard: they are both accessible and delightful to look at. A professional designer, she has a highly developed sense of colour and has gradually worked her way towards a predominance of pinks, soft mauves, yellows and white among the flowering plants. But she shows equal skill in her handling of foliage colouring, form and texture. Both she and her husband care very much for scented plants and have a special affection for their honeysuckle, jasmine and wistaria.

They have whittled down their tools to an amount which can be stacked neatly beside the door into the garden and keep their mower in a neighbour's shed. They use hand shears, a fork with small prongs and a long handle which minimises the need for bending, a spade for transplanting and a hand trowel and fork. Mrs Palin weeds directly into a basket and bags up bulky amounts of rubbish in plastics household sacks.

In the spring, they wait until the perennial plants are beginning to show before turning over all the soil. The garden then gets a feed of bonemeal, hoof and horn, and peat. This is topped up later on with liquid manure and one of the special proprietary rose foods. The maintenance routine goes quiet once the autumn leaves have been dealt with. Both of them find it too damp and cold to be out of doors during the winter months although they do choose plants which continue to make the garden look interesting from the house whatever the time of year.

Case history 3

Mrs Rose Hilleary began her garden 12 years ago beside a ground-floor flat converted from a Victorian terraced house near the Regent's Park Canal in London. The garden was an almost featureless stretch of wasteground 13 × 14m. But it faced south by west and was sheltered from the north and east by the terrace of houses, and from the west and south by brick walls. She hoped to make of it 'an unstylised, rather careless garden, crammed with my favourite shrubs, full of colour and scents'.

To begin with it consisted of one gnarled blackened robinia stump a few metres high, a neat little holly bush which reached up to her shoulder, and a mixture of rubble and soil which rose up towards the southern boundary. Beyond there was an area of undeveloped land on which grew a Lombardy poplar and two fine ash trees. These became a focal point in her plan.

The garden is more or less rectangular, though wider than it is long and she decided to organise it around a north-east/south-west axis which would lead the eye out towards the trees. To begin with, she called in a firm of garden designers to draw up a plan. When it arrived it came with an estimate for digging, and excavating the topsoil, but not for providing or putting in plants. 'The whole question immediately settled itself – I couldn't afford it. And anyway, I didn't like their plan. I'd seen that garden a hundred times.'

So she decided to work out the design herself. She used the slope to create a change in levels. There was already a terrace immediately outside the French windows extending into a little dog-leg on the north-west side of the living-room. It is all surfaced with crazy paving, 'the landlord's choice, certainly not mine'. She planned a small retaining wall 450mm high beside the terrace, and capped it with a stone coping. Since the boundary lines were all completely straight (with a bite taken out for an as yet unbuilt garage) she extended the wall in a curve alongside the holly. Two steps were let into this curve to lead up to the higher level.

Mrs Hilleary then hired a contractor to dig out the rubble, level the remaining soil and top it off with fresh topsoil brought in from outside. 'I think they just pushed the rubble around and covered it over, because I still find chunks of outhouse foundation at about 18 inches. I didn't even have any idea whether the topsoil they brought in was any good.' The contractors finished off by pegging out the site according to her plan of large curved planting areas, with lawn in between.

She ordered masses of plants, especially shrubs and shrub roses because the space looked so enormous. She had them planted during a particularly inclement October. 'The clay felt lumpy and unpromising and the plants looked miserable. I wondered if I had overdone the curves.' She had no idea how high anything would grow.

The following year she discovered two unpleasant things. The first was that south-westerly winds have such an uninterrupted line of attack until they hit the row of terraced houses that the ferocious down-draught nearly tears out by the roots those plants next to her paved terrace. Those had to be staked and tied every season. But she has since learned to grow lower and more resilient things there. The second discovery was that the poplar and the ash trees were to be felled to make way for garages. Despite securing a preservation order, in the end she was unable to save them.

Amongst the successful plants from the first year (many died) were a variegated cornus, a bignonia, two philadelphus, *Euphorbia wulfenii*, *Helleborus orientalis*, peonies and shrub roses 'Fantin

Latour', 'Mme Pierre Oger' and 'Empereur du Maroc'. She planted a *Rosa filipes* 'Kiftsgate' against the robinia stump, the grey-leaved weeping pear *Pyrus salicifolia* 'Pendula' in the middle of her paved courtyard and a loquat, grown from a stone saved on a Portuguese holiday. She started it off in a pot and eventually transferred it to a nook against the south-facing wall. The loquat is now a substantial and handsome tree. Underneath the holly she packed in rue plants (*Ruta graveolens* 'Jackman's Blue') as tight as they would go. 'But in all this planting, I never gave the soil a thought.'

When the poplar and ash trees eventually came down she found herself overlooked by another row of terraced houses. 'Being overlooked is one of the worst things about a town garden; you end up in this awkward situation of trying to create privacy for yourself without entirely losing the sense of scale.' She re-established her privacy by planting an almond in the south-west corner. It is successful as a screen, but: 'It is too dark and solid and I wish I had chosen something like a willow.'

The garden has two distinct changes of character. The paved courtyard, the terrace and wedge-shaped portion of the bed that flanks the terrace enjoy the greatest concentration of scent and colour. There are soft-blue petunias, roses, clematis, *Viola cornuta* and a 10-year-old hedge of lavender which flanks part of the retaining wall. There are several terracotta pots: large ones filled with blue agapanthus, white regale lilies, golden hops, scented pelargonium (the leaves give off the scent when they are disturbed) and clumps of hosta. All this part has the feel of a garden from some much more southern country. But the rest, beyond the steps, changes to something much more characteristically English. The planting largely conceals the courtyard area, and although there is something in flower there throughout the summer, it is heavily dependent on foliage.

Plants cannot be treated like an inert building material; the tall tree *left* over which *Rosa filipes* 'Kiftsgate' sprawls so voluptuously is the 'neat little holly bush' that reached Mrs Hilleary's shoulder when she began work on the garden. In the foreground, lilies and nicotiana. This part of the garden, the furthest from the flat, is quite different in character from the paved area – with its profusion of flowering plants in containers.

Below left adjacent buildings are screened by a *Robinia pseudoacacia* and by the smaller *Acer negundo* 'Variegatum'.

Below the border closest to the living-room is planted for colour and scent, though the fierce down-drought gives the roses a hard life. Hostas in containers have a better chance of keeping their leaves free from the ravages of slugs.

Case history 4

Leonard Manasseh is an architect. He and his wife Sarah, together with the first three of their five children, moved into their house, which he designed himself, in 1959. The house stands on what was the kitchen garden of a late Victorian mansion in the heart of Highgate village. The grounds of the mansion sloped south-east towards Highgate cemetery which now abuts the Manassehs' garden wall. Their house and the adjoining one on the garden plot were developed simultaneously.

The disadvantage of the site is that the drop to the cemetery is quite steep – about 2m from the level of their garden – and the land to the southwest, as well as the north-west, is higher: these factors together with the amount of water which must have run up against the cemetery's boundary wall together cause slight but continual slippage.

The Manassehs give the impression that the garden almost designed itself. There were a number of mature trees which were a great bonus; two apple trees, a crab apple and quince on the southern side and a flowering cherry, an apple tree – and a bank full of lily of the valley – at the back. They also put in a *Magnolia × soulangeana*.

There was an immense rubbish tip which had digested the mess of ages from the kitchen garden and which had become so huge that it was not practicable to move it. They decided to make use of it by building a brick wall round it to a height of 600mm and filling in the full height with some of the enormous quantity of soil that had been removed when the house foundations were dug. It is planted with a variety of low-growing shrubs and herbaceous plants. Not all of them grow low naturally. Mrs Manasseh says: 'I wish more of them did, but since I usually accept gratefully whatever plants people give me, I seldom find out what they are and am none too sure how they will turn out. If they're too tall, I'm afraid I chop them down ruthlessly.' She now wishes there was more foliage contrast among the plants in this bed.

Another feature which was clearly there to stay was a rectangular sunken garden whose presence in a Victorian vegetable plot remains a mystery. Apart from a brick-edged oval bed in the centre

and a semicircular lip at the southern end, it was entirely featureless. The Manassehs developed it into a three-dimensional, abstract pattern, a juxtaposition of hard surfaces – both horizontal and vertical – and simple, bold planting. There is a brick ziggurat in one corner ('it had to be topped with something spiky like a pineapple to look right, and it was a long time before we discovered the yucca'), a curved wedge of clipped privet, a vast rounded bush of lavender, bricked-in circular containers for smaller plants and overlooking it, a silvery-white figure sculpted by Daphne Hardy.

This stands on an oval base, a completion of the semicircular 'lip' which the Manassehs bricked up, filled with concrete and topped with cobbles.

The Manassehs' children were getting on towards the age of bicycling and scooters when they

moved in, so to give them maximum mileage with minimal damage to the garden a path was laid round the perimeter using a mixture of brick and concrete slabs. The one intersection is formed by the path which leads straight from the front door, down the west side of the sunken garden towards the cemetery.

The house was built of 100-year-old brick from a church in Southgate. The paving is a mixture of York stone, dark red Southwater engineering brick and Blue Stafford. 'Unfortunately, we didn't take so much trouble over the foundations for the paving as we'd had to for the house and consequently they have distorted, and the surfaces are beginning to flake from frost.' A great deal of trouble was taken over the foundations in the sunken garden and the surface there is impeccable.

The one tree which was already there that couldn't be saved was a pear which stood beside what is now the entrance to the garden. Garages were to be built right next door to it and in the course of building, a vital root was cut, the hard surfaces were brought too close to the trunk of the tree and it died. So a plane tree was planted instead and grew to an incredible 10m within 12 years until it was snapped off in a storm. What remains is still a graceful tree.

Plant list

The plants in these lists are recommended because they can flourish under town conditions (no guarantee that they will all flourish under *all* town conditions – Aberdeen is a rather different kettle of fish from Crewe) and because they generally combine at least two, often more, desirable characteristics, such as attractive foliage, beautiful flowers, pleasing forms, fragrance, seasonal changes of colouring.

Far from being exhaustive, all the lists necessarily suggest no more than a few of the innumerable plants that might do well in town conditions. Do not hesitate to try others; but rather than waste your money, take advice from a reputable nursery or knowledgeable plantsman before taking an expensive plunge into the unknown. Since it is impossible to be exact about height, the trees are classified as 'small', 'medium' or 'large': loosely, 4.5–9m, 10–18m and over 18m.

Trees

Acer negundo: Box Elder of North America. Deciduous. Medium to large, fast growing. Leaves pinnate, three to nine leaflets.
A. negundo 'Aureo-marginata' leaves yellow in spring.
A. negundo 'Variegatum' leaves have irregular white margin.

Ailanthus altissima: Tree of Heaven. Northern China. Deciduous. Large, fast growing. Large pinnate leaves similar to the ash. Tolerates atmospheric pollution well, colours shades of red in autumn and has conspicuous bunches of pods.

Catalpa bignonioides 'Aurea': Indian Bean Tree. USA. Medium sized, slow growing. Flowers (July/August) white with yellow and

purple markings. Leaves large – and in this variety, a striking shade of yellow throughout the summer –

appear late (May/June). Flowers followed by long, thin pods like straight runner beans.

Cotinus coggygria: Venetian Sumach or Smoke Tree. Central and south Europe. Deciduous. Small tree with rounded leaves whose flowers are so massed but so delicate that they appear like puffs of rose-coloured smoke.
C. coggygria 'Royal Purple' has deeply coloured leaves through most of the season, changing to dark translucent red in autumn.

Cydonia oblonga: Common Quince. North Persia and Turkestan. Deciduous. Small mop-headed tree with white flowers in spring followed by large, sweet-smelling fruit in autumn (good for jams and preserves and for cooking with pork).

Eucalyptus: Gum Tree. Australia. Evergreen. Fast-growing, susceptible to strong winds. Most species dislike

chalky soil. Often grown for glaucous colouring of young foliage.
E. gunnii: young leaves round and bluish, mature leaves sickle shaped and sage green. Very hardy.
E. niphophila: Snow Gum. Grows more slowly than other eucalyptus trees. Leathery grey-green leaves. Trunk is coloured with patches of cream, grey and green.

Fagus sylvatica 'Rohanii': deciduous. A purple-leaved form of the European Fern-leaved Beech. Potentially large but grows slowly. Dislikes heavy clay.

Gingko biloba: Maidenhair Tree, from eastern China. Deciduous. Sole survivor of a family that thrived 160m years ago. Medium-sized, slow-growing, columnar tree. Leaves, which resemble the Maidenhair Fern, turn yellow in autumn.

Tolerant of pollution and most soil conditions.

Gleditsia tricanthos: Honey Locust. USA. Deciduous. Tall, elegant tree with frond-like leaves but mature trunks frequently armed with sharp spines.
G. tricanthos 'Elegantissima': compact, slow growing.
G. tricanthos 'Sunburst' is without thorns. Young leaves are bright yellow.

Ilex aquifolium: Common Holly. Europe, north Africa and China. Evergreen. Small to medium tree.

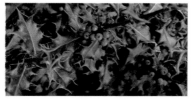

Hardy and tolerant of pollution.
I. aquifolium 'Bacciflava' has heavy crops of bright yellow fruit.
I. aquifolium 'Pendula': an elegant weeping form with red berries.

Juniperus chinensis 'Aurea': Young's Golden Juniper. Evergreen. The species is native to the Himalayas, China and Japan. 'Aurea' is tall but slow growing, conical or columnar, with golden foliage.

Koelreuteria paniculata: China Tree, Pride of India or Golden Rain Tree. China. Deciduous. Medium, wide-spreading, but delicate-looking tree. Pinnate leaves turn golden yellow in autumn. Clusters of small yellow flowers in July/August followed by conspicuous papery fruits. Easy-going tree in all soils.

Laburnum anagyroides: Common Laburnum. Central and southern Europe. A small tree with long drooping racemes of yellow flowers in late spring. Leaves tri-foliate and mid-green.
L. anagyroides 'Autumnale': sometimes flowers a second time. NB refer to list of poisonous plants on page 77.

Liquidambar styraciflua: Sweet Gum. Eastern USA. Deciduous. Unsuitable for shallow chalky soil but in other soils grows into tall handsome tree whose green maple-shaped leaves turn to bright crimson in autumn.

Liriodendron chinense: Tulip Tree.

Deciduous. This species, native of China and rarer than the North American type, is fast growing but of medium size. Unique leaf shape and exotic small greenish flowers.

Magnolia: China, Japan, Korea and USA. Deciduous and evergreen. Tolerant of most soil conditions, they like good living and require shelter

from wind and frost. Slow-growing, they take several years to flower but are aristocrats amongst flowering shrubs and small trees.
M. delavayi: China. Evergreen. Large shrub to medium tree, with enormous leaves, shiny above, glaucous beneath. Fragrant creamy-white flowers, late summer and autumn.
M. denudata: China. A small tree whose waxy lemon-scented flowers appear in April before the leaves.
M. sieboldii: Korea and Japan. Deciduous. Small elegant tree with large white flowers and conspicuous dark red stamens (May to August).
M. stellata 'Rosea': deciduous. A small tree, seldom more than 3m whose flower buds have a silky grey covering like smooth fur. Flowers (March) are profuse; the strap-shaped pink petals open out widely. The more commonly grown *M. stellata* has white flowers. Leaves mid-green.

Needs moist, fertile soil and shelter from north and east winds to prevent bruising of the petals.

Malus: the flowering crab apples are small to medium trees which tolerate

pollution and thrive in most soils. Flowering occurs in April/May and some varieties also fruit in the autumn.
M. 'Golden Hornet': white flowers followed by golden fruit.
M. 'John Downie': white flowers and orange/red fruit.

Metasequoia glyptostroboides: Dawn Redwood. China. Deciduous. Known to science as a fossil as late as World War II, it was 'rediscovered' in 1941. A vigorous, tall conical tree with shaggy red-brown bark. The small linear leaves are fresh green in spring, rose pink in autumn.

Pittosporum tenuifolium: New Zealand. Evergreen. Small tree, with small shining leaves, bright green with curly edges. Inconspicuous chocolate-coloured, vanilla-scented flowers in spring.

Pyrus salicifolia: Willow-leaved Pear. Caucasus. Deciduous. Graceful small tree, narrow silvery leaves, clusters of ivory-white flowers in spring. Tolerates cold and pollution.
P. salicifolia 'Pendula': a weeping form.

Robinia pseudoacacia: Common Acacia or Black Locust. USA. Deciduous. Fast-growing, tolerant of drought and pollution. Deeply furrowed bark and spiny twigs; attractive pinnate leaves and drooping racemes of sweet-scented white flowers. Its seeds are contained in shiny red-brown pods.
R. pseudoacacia 'Frisia': a popular

variety with golden-yellow leaves from spring until autumn.

Sorbus aria: Whitebeam. Europe. Deciduous. Small, compact tree. Native of chalk country. Simple grey-green leaves have luminous white downy undersides. Whole leaf turns golden in autumn. Clusters of white flowers followed by crimson fruit.
S. aria 'Lutescens': an outstanding variety, happy on most good, well drained soils, tolerant of pollution.

Sorbus aucuparia: Mountain Ash. Native. Deciduous. Familiar hedgerow tree in this country with delicate pinnate leaves, clusters of white flowers in early summer followed by bunches of small scarlet fruit.
S. aucuparia 'Xanthocarpa' has amber-yellow fruit.

Taxus baccata: Common Yew, a native plant. Commonly seen in churchyards because parishes were once obliged by law to grow them to make longbows and because the plant is so dangerous to animals that the churchyard was the only safe place when there were few other enclosures. The leaves are so dark that the effect is almost black. Compact dense shape. Slow-growing and tolerant of pollution.
NB refer to list of poisonous plants on page 77.

Shrubs

Sizes refer to approximate height and spread in that order.

Berberis: China, Japan, Europe and South America. Large family (over 400 species), both deciduous and evergreen. Deciduous foliage turns red in autumn. Evergreen forms have small glossy leaves and conspicuous small fruits – red, black, purple or blue. Evergreens will thrive in almost any site, sun or shade, if soil is reasonably fertile and well drained. Deciduous varieties need sun.
B. aggregata 'Barbarossa': west China. Vigorous shrub. Pale to mid-green leaves turn red and orange. Yellow flowers (July), then clusters of round coral fruits. Up to 2m.
B. darwinii: Chile. Small dark glossy leaves like holly, clusters of yellow flowers (April/May), blue berries. Good hedging plant; 3 × 3m.

B. thunbergii 'Atropurpurea': Japan. Red-purple foliage from spring until autumn; 1.5 × 2m.

Buddleia: America, Africa, Asia. Deciduous and evergreen shrubs and small trees grown for their plume-shaped or globular flowers. Need full sun.
B. davidii: Butterfly Bush. So named because butterflies are particularly attracted to the flowers (July-October). Varieties include 'Black Knight' (dark purple) and 'White Cloud' (pure white); 3 × 3m.
B. globosa: Chile. Semi-evergreen wrinkled leaves, orange-yellow globular flowers (May).

Buxus sempervirens: Box. Europe, west Asia, north Africa. Useful evergreen shrub which can be clipped into formal shapes, either free-standing or as low hedging.

Shiny oblong dark green leaves. Inconspicuous but scented flowers (April). Any reasonably drained soil, sun or light shade.

Camellia: India, China, Japan. Invaluable flowering evergreen shrubs which thrive in towns if soil is

fertile, moist and lime-free and position protected from wind. Choice is huge. White-flowered varieties include *Camellia* 'Cornish Snow'; *C. japonica* 'White Swan' or 'Lady Vansittart'. Pink-flowered varieties include *C. japonica* 'C M Wilson', *C. japonica* 'Fuoran', *C. reticulata* 'Butterfly Wings' and *C. reticulata* 'Donation'. Red-flowered varieties include *C. japonica* 'Fred Sander', 'Grand Sultan' or 'James Allen'. *C. reticulata* and its varieties may grow to 5m; *C. japonica* between 2 and 4m.

Caryopteris: east Asia. Deciduous small shrub (1m) with attractive silvery-green leaves and bright blue flowers in August/September. Ordinary garden soil, sunny position.
C. × clandonensis 'Ferndown': flowers violet blue.
C. × clandonensis 'Heavenly Blue': a more compact form.

Ceanothus: North America. Deciduous and evergreen. Outstanding shrubs; the majority have bright blue flowers in dense clusters and a long flowering season. Need good light soil and sunny

position. Deciduous forms can grow free-standing, evergreens need shelter of a wall.
C. arboreus 'Trewithen Blue': evergreen, with deep-blue flowers in spring.
C. 'Gloire de Versailles': deciduous. Powder-blue flowers (June/October). Can grow to 3m.

Cedrus libani 'Sargentii': evergreen. Small slow-growing form of the enormous Cedar of Lebanon. This is a prostrate variety with weeping branches. Ordinary well drained soil, preferably in sun.

Chaenomeles: China and Japan. Related to the quince (*Cydonia oblonga*, see tree list on page 66).

Useful deciduous shrubs, able to grow in sun or shade; in borders or against a wall. Attractive bowl-shaped flowers in spring and early summer followed by fruits in autumn; 2 × 2m.
C. speciosa 'Crown of Gold': crimson flowers, golden stamens.
C. speciosa 'Nivalis': large pure-white flowers.
C. × superba 'Knap Hill Scarlet': bright orange-scarlet flowers in profusion.
C. × superba 'Pink Lady': dark pink buds opening to rose-pink flowers.

Choisya ternata: Mexican Orange Blossom, native of Mexico. An invaluable, undemanding evergreen shrub, 2 × 3m. Thrives in any good

garden soil; prefers sun but tolerates light shade. White flowers, like a sober version of orange blossom, with an almost sickly scent (May).

Cotoneaster: China and the Himalayas. Grown for the brilliant autumn colour of the leaves or fruits. A tough and adaptable family, tolerant of most sites and soil conditions. Both deciduous and evergreen. Shrubs range from prostrate types to large bushes.
C. franchetii: graceful arching evergreen shrub, 2.2m, grey-green foliage, pink and white flowers (June). Orange-red berries. Suitable for hedging.
C. horizontalis: Herring Bone Cotoneaster. Deciduous shrub. Can grow to 3m against a wall, but as ground-cover remains under 1m and

spreads to 2m or more. Packed densely with red berries in autumn.

Cytisus: Broom. Europe, north Africa, Asia Minor. Popular shrubs, members of the pea family with small Sweet-pea-shaped flowers. Prefer full sun and well drained soil.
C. albus: White Broom. A bushy species up to 2m with slender arching branches covered in white flowers (April/May).
C. × praecox: Warminster Broom. Arching shape combined with profusion of cream-coloured flowers (April/May). Looks like an exploding firework in the height of the flowering season.
C. scoparius 'Johnson's Crimson'. Variety of the Common Broom with clear crimson flowers; 2.5m.

Daphne: Europe and Asia. Small to medium evergreen and deciduous shrubs with clusters of small, sweet-scented tubular flowers. They thrive in sun or partial shade in well drained soil: lime-tolerant.

D. mezereum: deciduous. Purple-red flowers (February) on bare stems followed by poisonous scarlet berries; 1.5m.

D. odora: evergreen with pale purple flowers (January-April) pleasantly scented. Needs protection from extreme cold. Up to 2m.

Elaeagnus pungens 'Maculata': the species is Japanese. Grown primarily for its foliage, this evergreen variety has butter-yellow splashes on its shiny green leaves. Up to 3m and not fussy about soil or position.

Enkianthus campanulatus: Japan. A deciduous shrub, 2.5 to 3m, with erect leaves and branches; clusters of tiny bell-shaped flowers, creamy yellow to bronze (May). Leaves turn red in autumn. Prefers neutral to acid soil, and a sheltered, slightly shaded position.

Erica: the heathers, all evergreen, vary from low ground-cover to tall shrubs (as much as 6m in the south-west). Species hardy in the UK originate in west Europe and the Mediterranean. The tenderer majority are from South Africa. Best grown in peaty, acid soils in an open position.

E. arborea: hardy species suitable for hedging. Faintly scented ash-white flowers (March/April).

E. cinerea: Bell Heather. Hardy compact plant (300mm); deep green leaves and white flowers (June-October).

E. × darleyensis: less than 1m, fully hardy, lime-tolerant. White, purple or pink flowers (December-May).

E. vagans: Cornish Heath, 1m. Pink flowers (July-December) and mid-green leaves. Tolerates mildly alkaline soil.

Fatsia japonica: Japan. Exceptionally handsome evergreen shrub with outstanding foliage. Hardy in the south. Fertile soil, sun or shade.

Forsythia: east Asia and south-east Europe. Too popular by half; every town garden has one and the result is a monotonous surfeit of blazing yellow in spring. Utterly

undemanding, stiff-looking deciduous shrubs.

F. × intermedia 'Spectabilis': very bright yellow (March/April). Can be grown as a hedging plant.

F. suspensa fortunei: may reach 4m against a wall. Bright yellow flowers (March/April).

Genista: Broom. Europe and north Africa. Easy-going family with all the grace that forsythias lack, whether low ground-cover plants or tall upright shrubs. Require ordinary light soil and generally need sun.

G. aetnensis: Mount Etna Broom. Delicate structure of rush-like branches on a woody trunk. A cloud of golden-yellow Sweet-pea-shaped flowers (July/August).

G. hispanica: Spanish Gorse. A dense spiny shrub, 1.2m, whose golden-yellow flowers (June/July) often obliterate the deep green foliage.

G. lydia: up to 1m. Spreading plant with arching grey-green branches and yellow flowers (May/June). Ideal for trailing over walls.

Halimium: Mediterranean region. Attractive small evergreen shrubs. Related to cistus, the flowers are very similar in shape but yellow. Plant in full sun, in a position sheltered from wind. Any light well drained soil.

H. lasianthum formosum: the purple-brown blotch on the petals forms a scolloped circle towards the centre of the flower. Grey-green leaves; 1 × 1.5m.

H. ocymoides: golden-yellow flowers with chocolate blotches at base of petals which form a distinctive dark centre.

Hebe: New Zealand. Underrated group of shrubs, the best of which have handsome foliage and dense spikes of flowers (usually lavender-blue or white) with a long season. Need shelter and full sun, but any well drained soil.

H. 'Carl Teschner': up to 300mm with 1.5m spread. Grey-green leaves on dark stems, 25mm spikes of violet-blue flowers.

H. macrantha: small shrub with glossy light green leaves. Flowers larger than other hebes, glistening white (June).

H. 'Midsummer Beauty': can grow

up to 3 × 4m. Long lavender flower spikes throughout summer. Reddish undersides to otherwise undistinguished leaves.

H. 'Pagei': 250 × 1000mm. Small glaucous leaves are attractive all year. Small spikes of white flowers (May/June).

Helianthemum: Rock-rose, from the mountains of central and southern Europe. Low-growing, vigorous evergreen shrubs which blaze with cistus-like flowers during summer. Any well drained soil, full sun.

H. lunulatum: grey leaves and bright golden flowers.

H. nummularium 'Beech Park Scarlet': crimson-scarlet flowers.

H. nummularium 'The Bride': white flowers.

H. nummularium: 'Wisley Pink': soft-rose-pink flowers.

Hydrangea: world-wide distribution. Popular deciduous and evergreen shrubs which respond to generous feeding and moist soil. Large-leaved varieties need some shade. The colour of blue and pink-flowered

forms is affected by acidity and alkalinity. Acid conditions intensify blues, turn pinks to blue and red flowers to purple. Alkaline conditions turn blue flowers pink and red flowers deep red. Neutral soil can produce full colour range. White hydrangeas are unaffected either way.

Hydrangea macrophylla: (2–3m) embraces two large deciduous groups, the hortensias, or mop-head hydrangeas and the lacecaps. Hortensias include:

H. macrophylla 'Deutschland': deep pink flowers.

H. macrophylla 'Générale Vicomtesse de Vibraye': bright rose or strong blue.

H. macrophylla 'Holstein': bright blue in acid soil.

Lacecaps include:

H. macrophylla 'Blue Wave': blue centres with pinkish-blue surrounds.
H. macrophylla 'Lanarth White': blue or pink centres with white surrounds.
H. macrophylla 'Mariesii': rosy pink.

Other types include:
H. paniculata 'Grandiflora': 3–4m, a superb deciduous shrub with large pyramid-shaped panicles of creamy-white flowers that age into papery transparency.

Jasminum nudiflorum: Winter Flowering Jasmine. China. Hardy deciduous shrub that needs support. Bright yellow flowers produced on naked dark green stems throughout winter and early spring. Will survive in almost any position and ordinary soil.

Juniperus: Juniper. World-wide distribution. Tough, slow-growing conifers which tolerate dry and alkaline soils. Two useful ground-covering species:
J. horizontalis 'Wiltonii': north-east America. Up to 300mm with spread of 2m. Blue-green awl-shaped leaves on long prostrate branches. Known as 'Blue Rug'.
J. procumbens: Japan. Similar, but grey-green colouring.

Lavandula: Lavender. South Europe. Grown in gardens for centuries for its fragrant flowers and aromatic foliage. Hardy, evergreen (the foliage is silvery grey), plants need replacing every six or eight years to prevent 'legginess'. Sunny position, well drained soil. Suitable for low hedges (600 × 600mm).
L. spica 'Hidcote': a compact form of old English lavender but with larger, darker violet flowers.
L. stoechas: French Lavender. Dense clusters of dark purple flowers topped by tufts of paler purple bracts.

Mahonia: China and USA. Superb shrubs, with exceptionally striking evergreen foliage and fragrant flowers. Any good soil, sun or shade.
M. aquifolium: Oregon grape. Glossy, leathery dark green leaves, thick clusters of creamy-yellow scented flowers (March/April) followed by blue-black berries.

M. japonica: China. 3 × 4m. Spiny dark green lanceolate leaflets, drooping sprays (150–250mm) of creamy-yellow flowers scented like Lily of the Valley (January-March). Blue-black berries.
M. lomariifolia: China and Formosa. 4 × 2m. Outline is like a rather stiff palm tree or a sweep's brush. Flowers January to March. Needs shelter.

Olearia haastii: New Zealand. One of a family of 100 species which generally do best in coastal regions. *O. haastii* is more tolerant of atmospheric pollution. Small glossy evergreen leaves are felty white below. White flowers like daisies occur in profuse terminal clusters (July/August). Well drained soil and a sunny, sheltered position; 2 × 3m.

Philadelphus: Mock Orange. Vigorous, unfussy deciduous plants that need a firm hand to keep them under control. White flowers, freely produced, are richly scented. Ordinary garden soil, sun or part shade; 1.8–2.4m. Some of the best named hybrids include:
P. 'Avalanche': masses of single flowers, slender branches.
P. 'Belle Etoile': flowers have a maroon flush at the centre.
P. 'Burfordensis': large single cup-shaped flowers have prominent yellow stamens.

Phlomis fruticosa: Jerusalem Sage. Mediterranean evergreen. 1 × 0.5m. Grey felty leaves, ripe-yellow hooded flowers in whorls. Needs sun and light soil.

Pieris formosa forrestii: China. Compact evergreen shrub of great merit. Young leaves are fiery copper red. When shrub matures, they combine with an abundance of small waxy white flowers in drooping clusters. Needs good lime-free soil and partial shade. Up to 4 × 5m.

Potentilla fruticosa: deciduous. Useful as a small flowering hedge (1.5 × 1.5m). Small open five-petalled yellow flowers appear in succession from May throughout the summer.

ROBERT ADAMS

Needs light soil and sun. Among the attractive named varieties:
P. 'Tangerine': flowers open a soft orange and fade to yellow.
P. 'Vilmoriniana': silvery foliage, ivory-white flowers.

Pyracantha: Firethorn. Asia and south Europe. Evergreen. Best as a wall shrub where there is room to let

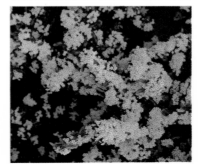

it look after itself since its star attraction is swags of brightly coloured berries, sustained throughout the winter. Their development would be impeded by pruning. Also smothered in white hawthorn-like flowers (May/June). Any well drained soil, sun or shade.
P. atalantioides: deep green leaves, crimson berries.
P. crenulata 'Flava': mid-green leaves, bright yellow berries.

Rhododendron: predominantly Himalayas, China, Tibet, India. A massive group of showy plants, that includes azaleas. Difficult to use well in town gardens since they look far more at ease in a woodland setting. Best to choose those with interesting leaf textures since dull rhododendron

foliage is overwhelmingly oppressive and the pyrotechnic flowering period may be brief.

Rhododendrons are intolerant of chalky soil. Well drained soil enriched with leaf mould or heavy soil lightened with peat are both suitable. Sheltered positions in half shade are ideal. Plants must not be allowed to dry out.
R. bureavii: 2 × 2m. Leaves dark green with furry red undersides. Clusters of pink flowers, speckled red (April).
R. campanulatum: up to 4 × 4m.

Leaves dark green above, woolly brown beneath. Flowers (April) pale lavender to purple.
R. concatenans: 2 × 2m. Young leaves are a smoky-blue colour, apricot-coloured flowers (April/May).
R. decorum: up to 3 × 3m. Grey-green leaves with smoky-blue undersides. Fragrant white flowers (March-May).
R. thomsonii: 3 × 2m. Leaves lustrous dark green above, glaucous beneath. Flowers (March/April) bell-shaped, waxy in texture and clear blood red.

Azaleas (correctly listed as Rhododendron):
Rhododendron arborescens: North America. Up to 5m. Deciduous shrub, leaves bright green on top, grey and hairy beneath. Cream, scented flowers (June/July).
R. kaempferi: 2.5 × 2.5m. Not quite deciduous. Dark green foliage. Flowers (May/June) vary from salmon pink or apricot to brick red.
R. luteum: 3 × 2m. Pale green leaves turn scarlet in autumn. Richly scented butter-yellow flowers (May/June).
R. schlippenbachii: deciduous shrubs whose fresh, pale leaves begin to appear at the same time as the clear-pink flowers (April/May). Up to 4 × 3m.

Rosa: if roses are to be grown primarily for their flowers, best to select a repeat-flowering form and place it in a border so that its ugly lower half is disguised by foreground planting. But don't overlook the less frequently grown species roses and some of the older forms which may

have both unusually attractive foliage and also glossy, decorative hips. Roses generally dislike shade, draughts and very poor soil. They need an annual feed.
This is a necessarily brief list.

Consult a specialist nursery (eg John Mattock of Oxford) for a wide choice of all kinds of roses, including the more rarely grown species, Albas, Bourbons, Damasks, Gallicas etc. Any and every garden centre can provide a selection of modern hybrid teas.

Species include:
R. × highdownensis: single deep-pink flowers (June) followed by spectacular flask-shaped red hips; 3 × 3m.
R. rubrifolia: dark red stems, smoky-purple foliage, modest pink flowers (June) and mahogany-red hips; 2.5 × 2m.
R. virginiana: glossy foliage turns fiery shades in autumn. Bright rose-pink single flowers, crimson hips.

Hybrid Musk Roses (outstanding for their fragrance) include:
'Buff Beauty': apricot-buff double flowers in clusters (June). Bronze-green foliage.
'Cornelia': sprays of small double flowers in various shades of apricot. Almost continuous flowering.
'Moonlight': dark green foliage, creamy-white semi-double flowers, bronze wood.

Repeat-flowering shrub roses include:
'Florence Mary Morse': an old floribunda type, free-flowering, with semi-double, crimson-scarlet flowers.
'Golden Wings': fresh pale foliage, large single golden-yellow blooms, sweetly scented.
'Nevada': dense first flowering (June) of large creamy-white flowers with golden stamens. Sparser subsequent crop.

Rugosa roses, which have distinctive heavily veined foliage include:
'Blanc Double de Coubert': large double white flowers, very fragrant. Long flowering season.
'Roseraie de l'Hay': large double flowers, soft crimson purple. Compact fragrant shrub.
'Schneezwerg': small, pure-white, semi-double flowers recur throughout summer, followed by scarlet hips.

Sarcococca confusa: Christmas Box. China. Useful evergreen shrub for ground cover in shade. Small tapering elliptic leaves;

inconspicuous flowers in winter are deliciously fragrant. About 1.5m. Any fertile soil, including chalky soils.

Senecio laxifolius: New Zealand. Special attraction is the distinctive soft silver-grey foliage (evergreen). Yellow daisy-like flowers (June/July). Prefers sunny sheltered position on well drained soil.

Skimmia japonica: Japan. Very adaptable, slow-growing evergreen shrubs (1.5 × 2m) which tolerate shade and pollution. Grown both for their compact rounded shape and long-lasting scarlet berries. Male and female flowers are produced on separate plants so both must be grown to produce fruits. Flowers (April) small, white and star-shaped. Chalky or acid soils.

Syringa: Lilac. Eastern Europe and Asia. Deciduous shrubs and small trees that thrive in town conditions. Most popular forms (varieties of *S. vulgaris*) are not very exciting except when in flower (May/June). Any fertile soil, sun or partial shade.
S. × persica: Iran to China. A graceful species with slender branches, lanceolate leaves and tapering lilac flowers. Makes a rounded bush 2 × 2.5m. Variety 'Alba' has white flowers.
S. vulgaris: varieties vary in height

from 2.5 to 4m. Heart-shaped leaves. Fragrant flowers in pyramid-shaped panicles. Named varieties include *S. vulgaris* 'Firmament' (soft lavender-blue flowers); *S. vulgaris* 'Primrose' (primrose-yellow flowers); *S. vulgaris* 'Souvenir de Louis Späth' (wine-red flowers); *S. vulgaris* 'Vestale' (pure-white flowers).

Viburnum: Europe, China, Japan, USA. Widely distributed family of attractive shrubs, both deciduous and evergreen. The flowering season of different species spans the greater part of the year. Some have attractive berries, others good autumn colour. Easy-going in most types of soil (it must be moist). Sun or part shade.
V. × bodnantense: 3.5 × 3.5m deciduous shrub. Stiff upright twigs and branches bear very fragrant rose-tinted flowers from December to February. Young foliage is slightly bronze coloured.
V. carlesii: 1.5 × 1.5m. Deciduous rounded shrub, ovate leaves, white flowers with delicious fragrance (April/May), black berries.
V. davidii: 1 × 1.5m Evergreen shrub with prominently veined, dark green

leathery leaves. Makes attractive low shape. Needs both female and male plants to produce striking turquoise-blue berries.
V. opulus 'Sterile': 4 × 4m. Deciduous, with large snowball-shaped flower heads (May/June) that open green and turn milky white. Red berries in autumn.
V. tinus: Laurustinus. Invaluable evergreen, 6.5 × 6.5m, with pink-budded, flat-headed white flowers throughout winter.

Climbers

Actinidia kolomikta: China, Japan. Deciduous plant, attractive mid-green heart-shaped leaves are splashed at the tips with white flushed pink. Needs good rich soil, well drained; sun or shade.

Clematis: incomparable group of evergreen and deciduous climbers with flowering seasons that span the entire year. Widely dispersed from Europe to China, the best known native plant is *Clematis vitalba* (Old Man's Beard). Clematis prefer to grow with their roots moist and in shade but their heads in the sun. Their successful cultivation requires some basic knowledge: refer to reliable nurseries and their catalogues such as Treasures of Tenbury.

Species clematis include:
C. armandii: a vigorous evergreen with leathery dark green leaflets in groups of three. Creamy-white flowers (April/May). Needs a warm, sheltered position.

C. cirrhosa balearica: Fern-leaved clematis. Attractive divided leaves become bronze in winter. Flowers are pale greenish yellow, spotted with red, throughout winter.

C. macropetala: deciduous plant with lavender-blue flowers followed by silky seed heads.
C. montana: rampant deciduous climber which will brave the chilliest conditions. White flowers (May). *C. montana rubens* has pale pink flowers and bronzed foliage.
C. tangutica: deciduous and exceptional for its lemon-yellow flowers (August/October) with petals as thick as lemon peel. Silky seedheads.

Large-flowered garden clematis are very showy but often more difficult to establish. They need richly endowed soil and an annual feed.
C. 'Ernest Markham': brilliant red (June-September).
C. 'Hagley Hybrid': shell-pink flowers (June-September) with brown anthers.
C. 'Henryi': immense white flowers (May/June) with dark stamens.
C. 'Lasurstern': clear lavender blue (May/June).
C. 'Marie Boisselot': large pure-white flowers (May/October) with cream stamens.
C. 'Mrs Cholmondeley': large pale blue flowers (May/August). Vigorous.
C. 'Mrs George Jackman': creamy-white flowers with brown stamens. Long flowering season.

C. 'Vivyan Pennell': astonishing double flowers in clear lavender blue.

Hedera: Ivy. Evergreen. If any plant is gardener-proof, it is ivy. Because it is familiar and unstoppable under any conditions, it is probably rather underrated. Use it to climb and to cover the ground. There are many readily available varieties, a number with variegated leaves that combine white or yellow with the more usual dark green.

Hydrangea petiolaris: Japan. Beautiful deciduous climber with fresh green leaves and flat-headed white flowers (June). Vigorous and happy in shade. Dislikes dry soil.

Jasminum officinale: Common White Jasmine. Persia, India, China. Attractive leaves composed of five to nine leaflets but grown for its deliciously scented tiny star-like white flowers. Needs warm sheltered position.

Lonicera: Honeysuckle. Evergreen and deciduous plants. Widely dispersed throughout the world and a familiar plant in native hedgerows. Like clematis, prefers its roots in damp shade and flowers in sun.
L. japonica: 'Aureoreticulata': semi

evergreen, leaves have conspicuous golden veining. Rampant growth, can reach 6m.

Parthenocissus henryana: Chinese Virginia Creeper. Best grown on a wall in half shade. Attractive deciduous leaves (three to five leaflets) dark green with pink and white highlights in the veining; they turn red in autumn. Needs to be planted in thoroughly enriched soil.

Passiflora caerulea: Passion Flower. Brazil. Attractive evergreen dark green palmate foliage.

Extraordinarily complex flowers of greenish white and purple. Best in southern counties in warm conditions. Flowering performance is

ROBERT ADAMS

HARRY SMITH

HARRY SMITH

unpredictable. Young plants need winter protection.

Rosa: a brief selection of the innumerable excellent climbing and rambling roses. Most need a sunny position but a number of exceptions are included.
'Aloha': large double coral-pink flowers, long flowering season. Suitable for north-facing position.
'Bobbie James': a rampant white rambler. Large trusses of ivory-white musk-scented small flowers.
'Danse du Feu': repeat-flowering climber, orange-scarlet semi-double blooms, dark foliage. Suitable for a north-facing wall.
'Golden Showers': repeat-flowering climber, small yellow buds open to large flat flowers. Can grow on a north-facing wall.
'Iceberg': a climbing version of the excellent floribunda. Pure-white

flowers, foliage less coarse than many roses.
'Maigold': large semi-double fragrant flowers of rich yellow. Very thorny.
'Mme Alfred Carrière': repeat-flowering, small thick white blooms tinged pink. Tolerant of north- and east-facing walls.
'Mermaid': large single sulphur-yellow flowers and a thick mass of amber stamens.
'Schoolgirl': copper-apricot flowers shaded pink, shaped like hybrid tea blooms. Fragrant and a long flowering season.
'Zéphirine Drouhin': the thornless rose. Sweet-scented double carmine-pink blooms. Needs a warm but airy position.

Vitis vinifera: Grape Vine. Caucasus and Asia Minor. There are several ornamental varieties including 'Purpurea' (the Teinturier Grape) whose foliage is deep red in summer and purple in autumn.

Grapes are purple-black. Needs rich soil, not acid, in almost any position but it will need sun to ripen the fruits.

Wistaria sinensis: China. Superb deciduous climber with attractive leaves composed of 11 leaflets. Racemes of pea-like lavender-coloured flowers may be as much as 350mm long. Flowers are abundant and scented. *W. sinensis* 'Alba' has white flowers. Wistaria needs well prepared soil and some shelter. Takes a long time to establish but well worth waiting for.

Herbaceous Plants

The term is used to describe plants that die back to ground level each winter and renew themselves again each spring. So if you don't want your garden to look ravaged in winter, be sure to use them in combination with a good selection of shrubs.

Acanthus: Bear's Breeches. South Europe. Sturdy plant with good foliage and tall spikes of strange hooded flowers. Sun or light shade, deep well drained soil; plant in a position where it will not be disturbed.
A. mollis: 1m. Large shiny ovate leaves with wavy margins. Flowers white and purple (July/August).
A. spinosus: 1–1.5m. Deeply cut, spiny leaves. Flowers, similar to *A. mollis*, with green bracts.

Achillea: Yarrow. South and east Europe. Hardy plants with delicate fern-like leaves. Popular border varieties have heads of tiny clustered flowers.
A. filipendulina 'Coronation Gold': 1m. Flat heads of deep yellow flowers (July/September).

A. ptarmica 'The Pearl': 500mm. Small pompons of white flowers (July/September).

Agapanthus: African Lily. Southern Africa. The strap-shaped shining

dark green leaves form large clumps. The rounded heads of funnel-shaped blue flowers are produced on the ends of thick dark green stems. The 'Headbourne Hybrids' are more hardy than the species.

Alchemilla mollis: Lady's Mantle. Carpathians to Asia Minor. Delightful plant for the front of a border (300–500mm). The light green leaves are slightly hairy and moisture gathers in them in diamond-like droplets. A foam of lime-yellow flowers (June/August).

Anemone × hybrida: three- to five-lobed deep-cut leaves in large clumps. Simple, elegant flowers (1m) from August to October in pink or white on stiff stems. Resents disturbance once established. Part shade, any fertile soil.

Aquilegia vulgaris: Columbine or Granny's Bonnet. Charming flowers, characteristically funnel-shaped

with a long 'spur' at the end of each of the five petals. Foliage bluish green, similar to maidenhair fern though larger. Hybrids (up to 1m) produce flowers in a variety of colours – cream, apricot, salmon pink, blue. Sun or partial shade.

Bergenia cordifolia: Siberia. A rather coarse plant but valuable for its winter colour. Drooping clusters of lilac-rose flowers (March/April). Leaves rounded. Any soil.

Campanula: Bellflower. Northern hemisphere. An attractive family (300 species) varying from creeping ground-cover plants to tall border plants. Flowers – typically white or blue – are bell-shaped or star-shaped. Any well drained soil: sun or part shade.
C. glomerata: Europe. Clusters of deep blue-purple flowers carried erect on stiff stalks (May/October); 100mm.
C. persicifolia: Europe, Siberia. Evergreen rosettes of narrow leaves, and slender spikes of open bell-shaped flowers, white or blue (June/August). Up to 1m.
C. portenschlagiana: low-growing mat-forming plant with masses of heart-shaped leaves. Pale blue flowers (June/November). Likes shade.

Cheiranthus × allionii: Siberian Wallflower. Mid-green leaves make a good dense clump (400mm). Terminal clusters of bright orange flowers. Likes very well drained soil; dislikes acidity.

Cynara cardunculus: Cardoon. A massive plant (3–4m) related to the artichoke. Deeply cut silvery leaves, spiky flower heads (August) with electric-blue bracts. Needs rich well drained soil and sun.

Eryngium: handsome thistle-like plants, teazle-headed and with deeply cut, spiny leaves. Sunny position and

well drained soil.
E. alpinum: steel-blue flower heads surrounded by a prominent 'ruff' of bracts (July/September); 500–600mm.
E. maritimum: Sea Holly. Europe. Deeply cut holly-like stem leaves are silvery green. Cone-shaped bluish flower heads (July/September); 300–400mm.

Euphorbia: Spurge. A large and widely spread family which thrives in relatively poor soil. Insignificant flowers but conspicuous bracts.

Needs full sun and good drainage.
E. griffithii: Himalayas. Lanceolate soft-green leaves have pale pink mid-

rib. Flaming-red bracts (May/June); 600–750mm.
E. myrsinites: a trailing plant with small stiff blue-grey leaves that clothe the stem thickly. Terminal clusters of lemon-yellow bracts (March/April).
E. polychroma: brilliant spring show of brightest yellow bracts in terminal clusters on sturdy, bushy plants; 400mm.
E. wulfenii: vigorous shrubby evergreen plant, up to 1.5m. Blue-green leaves, big clusters of yellow-green bracts (May/July).

Festuca glauca: Pyrenees. An attractive grass that grows in neat clumps with stiff but very fine blue-green leaves. Needs a sunny site; 50m.

Geranium: Crane's-bill. Not to be confused with the popular scarlet-, pink- or white-flowered plant commonly grown in pots and correctly named pelargonium. Crane's-bills are strong border plants with distinctive foliage and free-flowering habit. Ordinary soil, sun or light shade.

ROBERT ADAMS

G. grandiflorum: Central Asia. Bushy clumps of mid-green leaves, deeply cut. Blue to purple flowers (June/July); 300mm.
G. sanguineum lancastrense: a variation on our native Bloody Crane's-bill, this has pale pink flowers (June/September) darkly veined. Spreading clumps of dark green leaves (100 × 400mm).
G. wallichianum 'Buxton's Blue': bright blue flowers with pale centres, mid-green leaves flecked paler green (July/September).

Helleborus: group that includes the Christmas Rose. Evergreen and deciduous plants, useful both for their preference for moist shady

positions and for early, protracted flowering seasons. Need damp but not wet soil.
H. corsicus: Corsica and Sardinia. Handsome evergreen with trilobed pale green leaves and large clusters of creamy-yellow flowers, tinged green (March/May); 650mm.
H. foetidus: Stinking Hellebore. Evergreen with dark, finely cut

foliage. Yellowish-green flowers (March/May): 600mm.

Hemerocallis: Day Lily. Trouble-free plants whose clumps of strap-like mid-green leaves eventually provide substantial ground cover.

Lily-shaped flowers produced in succession. Sun or light shade; good soil.
Named varieties include:
'Cartwheels': bright yellow.
'Hornby Castle': brick red.
'Pink Damask': pink with yellow.

Hosta: Plantain Lily. Grown primarily for the foliage which is slug-prone. So best grown in pots on a hard surface if watered regularly. Partial shade, moist but not wet soil.
H. crispula: Japan. Pointed broadly lanceolate leaves, mid-green in the centre, irregular white margins. Lilac flowers (August); 650mm.
H. sieboldiana: Japan. 700mm. Good examples of this plant have a strong bluish shade about their large greeny-grey corrugated leaves.

Iberis sempervirens: Candytuft. South Europe. Small, tough, bushy plant with narrow dark green leaves, smothered in snow-white flowers (May/June). Spreads freely, 200 × 650mm. Good on poor soils in sunny position.

Iris: a family that includes small spring-flowering plants grown from bulbs to large 'bearded' summer-flowering border plants grown from rhizomes. Bearded irises are well

suited to town conditions. Leaves are glaucous, sword-shaped. Flowers large and complex with pendulous lower petals known as 'falls'. Need

full sun and a neutral soil. Named varieties (1m) flower in May/June and include:
'Blue Drift': strong blue, golden beard.
'Carnton': red brown.
'Jane Phillips': pale blue.
'Silver Tide': white.

Lamium galeobdolon: Yellow Archangel. Europe. Ground-cover plant (150–450mm) which runs riot in almost any conditions. Yellow flowers in whorls (June/July), palish evergreen foliage.

Lilium: Lily. Spectacular plants, relatively easy to grow. Well suited to pot cultivation though 'legginess' is perhaps best hidden in a border. They generally like rich neutral soil, sun or partial shade.
L. canadense: Canada Lily. North America. Petals of the bell-shaped hanging flowers curve upwards. Yellow to apricot (July); 1–2m.
L. 'Limelight': vigorous plant, large fragrant lime-yellow flowers (July/August); 2m.
L. pardalinum: Panther Lily. California. Hardy plant with pinky-orange flowers flushed yellow and spotted with brown (July); 2m.
L. regale: China. Large fragrant

funnel-shaped white flowers (July); 1.5–2m.

Lunaria annua: Honesty. Rather coarse but freely flowering plant (April/June). Purple flowers, mid-green toothed leaves, attractive flat round seed-carrying 'discs'; 650mm.

Pachysandra terminalis: Japan. Tough evergreen, useful for ground cover. Rosettes of shiny green leaves. Insignificant white flowers; 300mm. Any fertile soil; shade. Sometimes reluctant to get established but vigorous when it does.

Rodgersia: plants cultivated primarily for their foliage. They like rich moist soil, shelter and some shade.
R. aesculifolia: China. Has leaves like a giant horse chestnut. Flowering plumes (July) in pink or white; 1–2m.
R. pinnata: China. Deeply veined pinnate leaves which sometimes turn bronze. White flowers tinged pink (July); 1–1.5m.

Ruta graveolens: Rue. South Europe. Feathery leaves, steely blue in colour. Small sulphur-yellow flowers in July. Needs full sun and well drained soil; 650mm.

Sedum: fleshy succulent plant. Many of this family need greenhouse protection but a number thrive out of doors, even in poor, dry soil as long as they have sun.
S. roseum: Rose Root. Northern hemisphere. So named because the dried root smells of roses. Closely packed glaucous blue leaves on thick stems. Pale yellow flowers (May/June); 300–400mm.
S. spectabile: China. Curious stiffly upright plant, thick pale green leaves and flat wide heads of rose pink flowers (September/October); 300–400mm.

Stachys lanata: Lamb's Lugs.

Middle East. Thick silky ovate leaves, silvery grey. Compact

spreading habit best encouraged by removing inconsequential flower spikes.

Tiarella cordifolia: Foam Flower. Another useful ground-cover plant. Low-growing clumps of maple-green (evergreen) leaves spread densely. Spikes of creamy-white flowers (May/June); 150–300mm.

Vinca: Periwinkle. Europe. Tough invasive evergreen ground-cover with glossy foliage and small bright blue flowers (March/July). Ordinary soil, partial shade.

Bulbs

Anemone blanda: Mountain Windflower. Greece. Small bright blue flowers (February/April) with pale centres. Delicate foliage; 150mm. Plant 40–50mm deep in full sun.

Crocus: tough, undemanding and very rewarding. Plant 50mm deep, ordinary soil, any position.
C. chrysanthus: Greece, Turkey. Short narrow leaves, yellow-gold flowers (February). Parent of the following:
C. chrysanthus 'Blue Pearl': pale blue with white in the heart.
C. chrysanthus 'E A Bowles': bright yellow streaked with bronze.
C. chrysanthus 'Snow Bunting': white inside with yellow heart, streaked dark purple outside.

Cyclamen: Mediterranean. Very attractive small hardy relatives of the flamboyant pot plants. Need rich but well drained soil. Plant 25–50mm deep.
C. coum: south-east Europe. Leaves tend to be marbled in shades of green. Flowers (December/March) shades of pink, or white; 75mm.
C. neapolitanum: Italy, Greece. Variable leaves, occasionally with silvery markings. Flowers pale

mauve (August/November); 100mm.

Eranthis hyemalis: Winter Aconite. Bright lemon-yellow flowers, like kingcups; a 'ruff' of pale green leaves (February/March). Plant 25mm deep in moist but not wet soil, sun or partial shade.

Galanthus nivalis: Snowdrop. Europe. Familiar white bell-like flowers, green markings (January/February). Grows best in rich moist soil. Plant 50mm. May not establish itself easily.

Iris: the small spring-flowering irises prefer very well drained alkaline soil. Plant 50–75mm deep.
I. danfordiae: eastern Turkey. Bright butter-yellow flowers (January/February); 100mm.
I. histrioides 'Major': 100mm. Royal-blue flower (December/February).
I. reticulata: Russia, Caucasus. Dark purple flowers with an orange blaze (February/April); 150mm.

Narcissus: the daffodil family varies from the long-stemmed blooms produced commercially for cut flowers to very small spring-flowering types. Leaves of the former (which should be left for a long period after flowering) make the plant too untidy for small town gardens. The small early flowering species need a good moist position, full sun or part shade. Plant 50–75mm deep.
N. bulbocodium: Hoop Petticoat. South-west France. Wide open

butter-yellow flowers (February/March) and slender almost grass-like leaves; 50–100mm.

N. cyclamineus: Spain, Portugal. Dark linear leaves and slender tube-like flowers with swept-back petals (February/March); 150–200mm.

Tulipa: the popular border tulips are easily obtained and many are a crude development of these characterful

species. Tulips like alkaline soil. Plant 150mm deep.
T. clusiana chrysantha: yellow flowers, flushed red on the outside (April); 150–200mm.
T. kaufmanniana: Water-lily Tulip, Turkestan. Grey-green leaves, white flowers flushed red and yellow (March/April). Six petals open into a star shape; 150–180mm.
T. praestans 'Fusilier': central Asia. Grey green leaves and scarlet flowers (March/April); 150–250mm.
T. tarda: central Asia. Clumps of strap-shaped mid-green leaves. White flowers with bright yellow hearts (March); 150mm.

Poisonous plants

This list has been deliberately kept short because it is very easy to lose a sense of proportion about the subject. The fact is that cases of poisoning among humans from the accidental ingestion of toxic substances in plants are rare, and fatalities extremely rare. The simple reason is that the great majority of these plants taste so unpleasant that an adult or child would spit them out long before any damage was done. Also it should be remembered that plants that are poisonous to animals are not necessarily poisonous to humans. (Conversely the rabbit can digest sufficient quantities of the Death Cap Mushroom to wipe out three or four human adults without doing itself any harm.) If you would like to read a more extensive list, including plants that are neither commonly in cultivation, nor as readily found as these are, consult *British Poisonous Plants*, published by Her Majesty's Stationery Office.

If you ever do suspect that someone is suffering from poisoning after eating part of a plant, get medical help immediately and try to keep a sample of the plant, if you cannot identify it accurately.

Aconitum: Monkshood. All parts of the plant are poisonous, but the only human fatalities on record occurred because the root was dug up in mistake for horseradish (a good reason for not mixing vegetables and flowers in a small town garden).

Aquilegia: Columbines. An infusion of the seeds is used medicinally in several countries and this is dangerous to children.

Daphne mezereum: children might be attracted by the red fruits which can be sufficiently poisonous to be fatal.

Digitalis: Foxglove. The plant is highly poisonous yet there is no

record of human poisoning in this country for the past twenty years (only one of a flock of turkeys) because it tastes so unpalatable.

Euonymus europaeus: Spindle Tree. A shrub that grows to about 2m and has conspicuous small pink fruits in autumn which are acid, poisonous and purgative.

Euphorbia: the Spurge family all have a milky substance in the stem which can irritate the skin. The fruits on the so-called Caper Spurge (*E. lathyrus*) should not be confused with capers since the former contain an irritant poison.

Hedera helix: Common Ivy. Humans have been poisoned by ingesting ivy leaves but children are more likely to be attracted by the berries (also poisonous).

Hellebore: the Stinking Hellebore (*Helleborus foetidus*) and the Green Hellebore (*H. viridis*) are native to Britain, but many other kinds are common in gardens (*H. niger, H. orientalis, H. corsicus* etc). All parts of the hellebores are poisonous to men and animals.

Ilex aquifolium: Common Holly. The berries are poisonous.

Laburnum anagyroides: all parts of this small tree are poisonous and there are numerous cases of humans being poisoned from eating the

flowers or seeds, or merely from having held a twig in the mouth.

Lathyrus: Sweet Pea. Regarded

primarily as a danger to horses, it can also affect humans though most cases have occurred in countries where people have been forced to eat the plant through lack of food.

Ranunculus bulbosus: many members of the ranunculus family are to a greater or lesser degree poisonous but there is only one case on record of children suffering mild poisoning from chewing buttercup roots.

Rheum rhaponticum: Rhubarb. Only the pink stems should be eaten. The leaf, even if cooked, can harm humans.

Taxus baccata: Yew. All parts of the yew are poisonous except the

bright-red fleshy covering of the seed. But there is a risk that, attracted by its colour, a child might swallow the whole fruit, including the seed which is deadly. There have been a number of fatalities.

Nursery list

Bressingham Gardens
Diss
Norfolk IP22 2AB
Herbaceous plants

Broadleigh Gardens
Barr House
Bishops Hull
Taunton
Somerset
Small plants grown from bulbs

Chatto, Beth
White Barn House
Elmstead Market
Colchester
Essex
Both moisture-loving plants and those well suited to drought

Clifton Geranium Nurseries
Cherry Orchard Road
Chichester
Sussex PO19 2BX
Pelargoniums

Hillier Nurseries (Winchester) Ltd
Winchester
Hampshire SO22 5DN
Trees and shrubs, roses and herbaceous plants

Ingwersen W E Th Ltd
Birch Farm Nursery
Gravetye
East Grinstead
Sussex RH19 4LE
Alpines

Mattock, John Ltd
Nuneham Courtenay
Oxford
Roses

Notcutts Nurseries Ltd
Woodbridge
Suffolk IP12 4AF
Trees, shrubs and ground-cover plants

South Down Nurseries
Redruth
Cornwall
Trees and shrubs

Treasures of Tenbury Ltd
Burford House
Tenbury Wells
Worcestershire WR15 8HQ
Clematis

Treseder's Nurseries (Truro) Ltd
The Nurseries
Truro
Cornwall
Trees, shrubs and herbaceous plants; special knowledge of seaside conditions

Mrs D Underwood
Colchester
Essex CO4 5BD
Silver foliage plants

Book list

Design and Detail of Space between Buildings
Elisabeth Beazley
Architectural Press, 1960

The Easy Path to Gardening
Reader's Digest Association and the Disabled Living Foundation, 1972

Foliage Plants
Christopher Lloyd
Collins, 1973

Garden Design
Sylvia Crowe
Country Life, 1958

Hillier's Manual of Trees and Shrubs
David & Charles, 1972

The Nature of Landscape Architecture
A E Weddle (ed)
Heinemann, 1967

The Penguin Book of Basic Gardening
Alan Gemmell
Penguin Books, 1975

Reader's Digest Encyclopaedia of Garden Plants and Flowers
The Reader's Digest, 1971

Room Outside: New Approach to Garden Design
John Brookes
Thames and Hudson, 1969

Techniques of Landscape Architecture
A E Weddle (ed)
Heinemann, 1967

Trees and Bushes of Europe
Oleg Polunin
Oxford University Press, 1976

Variations on a Garden
Robin Lane Fox
Macmillan, 1974

The Well-tempered Garden
Christopher Lloyd
Collins, 1970

Acknowledgements

The author is grateful to the following for their help: Geoffrey Grant, advisor on the section 'Gardens and the law'; Miss M Chaplin, consultant to the Disabled Living Foundation; Robert and Marina Adams; Clifford Tandy; Simon Swaffield; Sally Visick. She is also grateful to the following for permission to quote from publications in which they hold the copyright: The Architectural Press Ltd for the extract from *Do-it-yourself Playgrounds* by M Paul Friedberg and *The Nature of Landscape Design* by Nan Fairbrother; Dame Sylvia Crowe and the Hearthside Press Inc for extracts from *Garden Design* by Sylvia Crowe; William Heinemann Ltd for two tables from *Techniques of Landscape* edited by A E Weddle; Macdonald and Jane's Publishers Ltd for an extract from *Gardens* by Peter Shepheard; Martin Secker & Warburg Ltd and the Viking Press Inc for an extract from *The Middle Age of Mrs Eliot* by Angus Wilson.